SASOL

OWLS &
OWLING

IN SOUTHERN
AFRICA

WARWICK TARBOTON
& RUDY ERASMUS

STRUIK

To Michèle, Zeta and the owlets
– W. Tarboton and R. Erasmus

Struik Publishers (Pty) Ltd
(A member of Struik New Holland Publishing (Pty) Ltd)
Cornelis Struik House
80 McKenzie Street
Cape Town 8001

Reg. No. 54/00965/07

First published in 1998

Project manager: Pippa Parker
Editor: Tracey Hawthorne
Assistant editors: Jenny Barrett and Helena Reid
Cover design: Dominic Robson
Designers: Dean Pollard and Dominic Robson
Proofreader: Annelene van der Merwe

Reproduction by Hirt & Carter (Pty) Ltd, Cape Town
Printed and bound by CTP Book Printers, Parow

ISBN 1 86872 104 3

Front cover: Cape Eagle Owl (top, left), Spotted Eagle Owl
(bottom, left), Pearlspotted Owl (right); **Spine:** Marsh Owl;
Back cover: Scops Owl.

10 9 8 7 6 5 4 3 2 1

CONTENTS

ACKNOWLEDGEMENTS

Over the years we have shared many pleasurable days owling, not only in each other's company, but also in the company of many friends and colleagues. To all of them, and to others who have responded generously to our requests for information, access to land, ideas and assistance in finding owls we extend our warmest thanks: Graeme Arnot, David Allan, Des and Jen Bartlett, Garth Batchelor, Keith and Colleen Begg, Sheila Blane, Adriaan Botha, Hendrik Botha, Piet Botha, Gerry Bowden, Gary Bronner, John Carlyon, Peter Chadwick, Jannie Coetzee, Ernst Conradie, Dave Cruse, Dick and Theo Daly, Sam de Beer, John Dunning, Rob Davies, Christo and Christie de Beer, Richard Dean, Denis Driver, Sieg Eiselen, Ben Erasmus, Theuns Erasmus, Zeta Erasmus, Walter and Topsy Eschenberg, Ernst Fisher, Peter Frost, Kobus Fourie, Ken Gamble, Ken Gordon, Doug Galpin, Richard and Barbara Galpin, Neil Greenwood, Erik Grimbeek, Johan Grobbelaar, Bob Haagner, Clem Haagner, Peter Haagner, Jonathan Haw, Pieter Henning, Kotie Herholdt, George and Ann Hodgson, John Hymans, David Johnson, Antoinette Jurgens, Alan Kemp, Johan Kloppers, Elna Kotze, Paul du P. Kruger, Hendrik Kroep, Elias le Riche, Stoffel le Riche, Anton Lindstrom, Geoff Lockwood, Billy Lombaard, Esme Loubscher, Roz Marais, Janet Matthews, John McAllister, John McGregor, Andrew McKenzie, John Mendelsohn, Johan Moolman, Rob Martin, Anton Muller, Flip Nel, Jock Orford, Bube Pienaar, Pondo Pienaar, Pieter Pieterse, Boet Potgieter, Glenn Ramke, Clive Ravenhill, Eddie Reineke, Marinda Richards, John Robinson, Scott Ronaldson, Neels Roos, Brendan Ryan, William Scott, Rob Simmons, Rob Slotow, Derek Solomon, Lorna Stanton, Peter Steyn, Dave Steyn, Don Stott, Guggi, Michèle and Mike Tarboton, Charles Taylor, James and Grace Thompson, Tony Tree, Jerry Theron, Ron Tucker, Wynand Uys, Willie van Aardt, Giel van der Merwe, Tuba van der Walt, Koos van Deventer Snr., Koos van Deventer Jnr., Huib van Hamberg, Petrus van Rensberg, Michel Veldman, Carl Vernon, Gerard Verdoorn, Willie Victor, Ivan and Prudence Visser, Mark Wagner, Margie Wagner, Ron Wagner, Hans Willemse, Alan Whyte, Ian Whyte, and Nick Zimbatis.

It was a pleasure to work with Pippa Parker and the editorial team at Struik Publishers on this book, and we gratefully acknowledge the loan of slides for the book from Keith Begg (Pel's Fishing Owl, pages 57 and 69); Kobus Fourie (Marsh Owl, page 42, and Barred Owl, page 59); Clem Haagner (Giant Eagle Owl, pages 8 and 54, Spotted Eagle Owl, page 25 *left*, Whitefaced Owl, page 44, Wood Owl, page 61 *bottom*) .

Encouraging owls to our neighbourhoods, learning about them, watching them and photographing them has given us enormous pleasure. Long may our owls continue to live and flourish and give joy to increasing numbers of people!

SPONSOR'S FOREWORD

The owl is widely perceived to be a source of great
wisdom. Sasol believes it is wise to care for our
environment and we therefore take pride in our association
with this delightful book on southern African owls.

We are convinced that this publication will enhance
the knowledge of and concern for these unique and
supportive raptors of the dark.

PAUL DU P. KRUGER
Chairman, Sasol Limited

Sasol and the Environment

*'Protecting our environment is an obligation
– not a choice'.*

Sasol believes that the quality of the air, water and soil
should be protected for the continued benefit of all
ecosystems. In this way, the needs of the present and
future generations will be met.

Sasol is committed to act responsibly and with due
regard to the effects of its operations and products on
the environment. Protecting the environment is an
obligation – not a choice.

Consequently, it is Sasol's policy to judiciously limit the
environmental impact of all its activities.

INTRODUCTION

There are surely few other groups of birds in the world as clearly etched in collective memories, folklore and legends as are owls. To some people, owls are simply birds that go about their business at night; or, at a more abstract level, they may be symbols of wisdom, scholarliness or absentmindedness. But to others, the word 'owl' has more sinister and frightening connotations: to them an owl may be the harbinger of bad news or evil spirits, not just in the cultures of many traditional African societies but also in western cultures that date as far back as the times of Aristotle, King Arthur and Shakespeare. Regardless of language, background or culture, therefore, the chances are that for most people owls conjure up vivid images in a way that few other birds or animals do.

Everyone knows what an owl is, but remarkably few people have ever really experienced owls. Most people have neither seen nor heard an owl, despite there being several common, widespread owl species in southern Africa (a number of which live in towns and cities) – and even though all owls leave obvious telltale signs of their presence.

We hope that this book will open up the world of owls to more people, that it will create an appreciation of owls and increase awareness of their comings and goings, and that it will help people to discover owls living nearby and give more thought to owls and their future.

Owls are found in virtually every corner of the globe, and our southern African owls are a microcosm of the owls of the world. Both the largest owls in the world (the eagle owls) and the smallest (the pygmy owls) are represented in the southern African region, as is the world's most abundant (the Barn Owl) and a representative of one of the more unusual groups (the fishing owls). We also have forest owls and grassland owls; sedentary, highly territorial owls; and wandering, highly nomadic owls. And, lastly, we have our own 'enigma owl': the coastal Barred Owl, first described from the Eastern Cape province in 1834 and not seen again for nearly 150 years, until its dramatic rediscovery in 1980.

There are 130 to 175 species of owl found worldwide. This disparity in the number of species arises not from the various owl taxa having been inadequately described, but rather from the taxonomic revolution that is quietly toppling the traditional concepts of what, exactly, species are.

A few years ago one may have been safe in stating that there were, say, 135 species of owl, but with increasingly sophisticated DNA studies being conducted on many avian groups, many more bird species are now being recognised as a result of the splitting of what were formerly regarded as single species. For this reason, 'between 30 and 40' is the closest we can get to the number of owl species recorded in sub-Saharan Africa. In the southern African region there are certainly at least 12 species, and perhaps when DNA techniques are applied to our owls, this tally will increase to 13 or 14.

CREATURES OF THE NIGHT

What sets owls apart from other birds is their ability to operate after dark, and it is this, their nocturnal lifestyle, that has intrigued man down the ages. Fewer than three percent of the world's birds are nocturnal, and most of these are owls. Their success in pursuing a low-light existence rests on their acute sight, fine hearing and ability to fly slowly and silently.

NIGHT EYES

Enormous eyes are one of the most characteristic features of owls and, coupled with their forward-looking faces, give these birds remarkably human-

The striking orange-coloured eyes of the Cape Eagle Owl.

HERE'S LOOKING AT YOU

How does owl vision compare with human vision? The eyes of the larger owl species are as big as (sometimes bigger than) those of an average human being, and comparative optical studies have been undertaken in one such species (the European Tawny Owl, a close relation of Africa's Wood Owl) in which the focal length of the eye (the distance from the lens at the front of the eye to the retina at the back) is very similar to that of the human eye. Tawny Owls' eyes differ from those of humans in having larger pupils (the pupil being the hole or 'aperture' that lets in light) – 13,3 mm in diameter compared to 8 mm in human eyes. In photographic language, the owls' eyes are 'faster' – their 'f-stop' is 1,03 compared to 2,13 in human eyes – and this enables the eye to receive a brighter image in low-light conditions. Claims sometimes made that owls can see 100 times better in the dark than humans are far off the mark; for this to be possible, owls would require eyes larger than tennis balls!

The 'absolute visual threshold' (the ability to detect low levels of light) of owls' eyes are also superior to that of human eyes by a factor of 2,2: owls can see in light conditions too poor for human eyes. By comparison, cats have an absolute visual threshold that is superior to both humans (by a factor of 5) and owls (by a factor of 2,2). (Cats' enhanced vision is partly the result of a reflective coating on the retina which increases light capture, and which causes the 'eye shine' that cats have).

A diurnal bird like a pigeon has eyes that are 100 times less sensitive than those of owls in their ability to detect light.

Scops Owl with pupils wide open to make effective use of poor light.

looking heads. Owls' eyes are not spherical like those of a human, but tubular in shape, a design that minimises weight – critical in birds – and at the same time has the effect of reducing the area of the retina and so reducing the owl's field of view. This is thought to be the reason for the unusual front-facing placement of the eyes, which is necessary to achieve binocular vision.

The forward-looking, human-like face of the Giant Eagle Owl.

Because of their restricted angle of vision, owls swivel their necks rather than their eyes to look in different directions, and can rotate their heads through 270° to 360° compared to a human's 180°. Their comical habit of bobbing and swaying their heads when focusing on an object is a mechanism owls have perfected for enhancing their three-dimensional view.

An owl's visual capabilities in poor light are a few times better than a human's, much better than a diurnal bird's, and a little inferior to a cat's (see box, page 7). Owls can accordingly cope with darkness considerably better than humans (it has been suggested that an owl can see as well in starlight as a human can in full moonlight), but their ability to distinguish detail falls off with diminishing light, and on totally dark nights (both moonless and starless) they are essentially as incapable of seeing as humans are.

Although they are primarily night birds, owls are not helpless during the day. Their pupils have an exceptional range, and can both open up to a high aperture in the dark and close down to a tiny pinprick in bright daylight. In fact, not all owls are equally nocturnal, and two southern African species (the Marsh Owl and the Pearlspotted Owl) are active by day. The closed-eye look that an owl may give an observer during the day is more to conceal its eyes and blend in with its surroundings than to shut out daylight.

In addition to eyelids, all owls have inner lids which protect the eyes, such as when they fly between close-set branches or bring food to vociferous chicks.

Finally, it is widely believed that owls have black and white vision. Tests done on at least two species have, however, shown that their eyes are receptive to colour.

HEARING

Acute hearing is the owl's second adaptation for coping with night life. It is less their ability to detect soft sounds (which is really not much higher than a human's) than their ability to judge where a sound comes from, that is considered impressive.

The Barn Owl listening intently for prey.

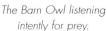

The facial disc of the Barn Owl acts as an effective sound reflector.

In the 1960s a researcher in the USA, RS Payne, conducted experiments to show how Barn Owls locate and catch prey in total darkness relying only on their hearing. Barn Owls specialise in hunting small rodents, and they catch these in the way of most owls, swooping gently down on them while in flight or from a perch and grasping them in their talons. The experiments involved a tiny microphone, emitting mouse-like rustling noises, being dragged across the leaf-covered floor of a large, totally dark room, on one side of which perched a Barn Owl. The owl was deadly accurate in its ability to locate the 'prey' up to a distance of about seven metres; beyond this, it would fly towards the prey and land, waiting for further auditory clues. If one of the owl's ears was plugged closed, its ability to judge angle and distance was greatly reduced. (The Barn Owl experiments also demonstrated that these birds neither hunt by scent nor are capable of detecting infrared radiation.)

An owl's ear openings are located on either side of its head, directly behind its eyes. They are large, and in some owl species they are asymmetrically positioned, one being lower than the other. In some species (including the Barn Owl) the openings are covered with thin skin flaps that can be adjusted according to the direction of the incoming sound.

All owls have facial ruffs. In the Barn Owl and the Grass Owl the ruff forms a dark fringe enclosing the bird's dramatic white face. Situated directly behind the ear openings, these stiff ruff feathers provide a sort of parabolic reflector, or 'ear trumpet', that focuses and amplifies incoming sound, and are the 'secret weapon' that enables owls to locate and accurately pinpoint the position of prey in the dark.

It may be a surprise to discover that owls do not differ significantly from humans in their ability to detect soft sounds. It has been proposed that the auditory systems of both humans and owls are close to the theoretical limits of sound detection and that any improvement in this direction would be wasted because of

The Grass Owl's ear openings are concealed below its ruff feathers.

A Grass Owl with chicks, one of which is swallowing its prey.

interference from ambient background 'noise', be it the sound of heartbeats, the rustle of wind or traffic noise.

ON SILENT WINGS

The last weapon in owls' armoury is their ability to fly silently. This, it is presumed, enables them both to approach prey without being detected and to hear optimally even when in flight. This silent flight is partly a product of the owls' downy-fringed flight feathers, and partly because of their low wing-loading (a lot of wing surface for such a light body).

In most birds, the edges of the flight feathers are finely barbed so as to hold the feather-edge together in flight and maximise lift potential. Lacking such feather barbs, owls have soft-edged flight feathers which muffle the sound of the wings beating. Owls are slow-flying, partly because of their low wing-loading and partly because of the added drag arising from less efficient flight-feather edges.

While slow flight has numerous advantages in nocturnal conditions, not all owls have the need for silent flight, and not all owl species fly silently.

CAMOUFLAGE

The plumage of most owl species is coloured and patterned to blend in with its surroundings, and an owl sitting quietly in its daytime hideout can be astonishingly difficult to find. The most impressive of the world's owls in terms of cryptic coloration is not a southern African species, but one found in the Arctic tundra. As white as a polar bear, the Snowy Owl can sit quietly in a hollow in a snowfield, blending with its environment to a remarkable degree.

The southern African species, with the exception of the pale *Tyto* owls, are all basically brown and/or grey, mottled, spotted, streaked or barred with lighter or darker tones that enable them to blend into their forest, savanna, grassland or desert environments.

During the day, some owl species perch pressed against the trunk of a tree, some hide in tangled creepers, and others retreat into dark holes, sitting with their feathers drawn tightly against their scrawny bodies to reduce their size, and with their eyes almost closed to minimise any telltale glint.

This daytime reclusiveness may give the impression that owls are like this all the time. At dusk, however, when they venture forth to hunt and find partners and breed, owls become far more conspicuous. They often perch prominently against the skyline, on rooftops, telephone poles and fence posts, or on rocks, and, especially before the onset of breeding, they become vocally active.

EGGS AND BREEDING SEASONS

Like owls the world over, southern African owls all lay plain white, smooth-surfaced eggs which are more rounded than those of most raptors. Although white eggs are conspicuous to predators and so seem maladaptive, owls seldom leave their eggs unattended – the incubating bird sits close and is not easily flushed off the nest, and her cryptic plumage camouflages her well. Furthermore, many owls nest in dark holes and are active mainly at night; in the darkness, white eggs are more easily located by a bird returning to its nest, so are less likely to be trampled on and damaged.

The two largest owls (the Giant Eagle Owl and Pel's Fishing Owl) normally lay a clutch of two eggs and, in common with most of their large-eagle counterparts, rear only one chick at a time. It is not clear to what extent this is the result of sibling aggression (as it is in eagles) or simply of the smaller nestling starving. Further similarities between these large owls and large eagles include their breeding during winter and their habit of alternating years of nesting with non-nesting. In these respects the large Cape Eagle Owl lies somewhere between these two large species and the other, smaller owls. It usually lays two eggs (sometimes three) and like most of the larger eagles breeds in winter. However, it normally rears both chicks from a clutch.

With the exception of the extraordinary Barn Owl (which can lay up to 19 eggs), owls typically lay two to five eggs. The small insectivorous owls (the Scops Owl, Pearlspotted Owl, Barred Owl and Wood Owl) usually lay two or three, while those species that prey mainly on rodents (the Grass Owl and Marsh Owl) lay three or four.

Of these smaller owls, the insectivores breed in early summer and the rodent-eaters mainly in early winter. The Whitefaced Owl and Spotted Eagle Owl spoil this neat pattern by eating mainly rodents and nesting in early summer!

CALLS OF THE NIGHT

The sound of an owl calling is one of the most characteristic noises of the night. In many urban locations it is the 'hu, hooo' or 'hu-hu-hoooo' hooting of the Spotted Eagle Owl or the shrill screech of the Barn Owl that cuts the night air. In bushveld country it is the ventriloquial 'prrrup' of the Scops Owl, or the piercing whistles of the Pearlspotted Owl, that is most likely to break into the cacophony of cricket noises. Near a marshy area the harsh, rasping 'gggg, k-k-k-k-k' of the Marsh Owl joins the sound of frogs.

A Spotted Eagle Owl hooting, showing a flash of white throat with each hoot.

This is how owls find partners, or, if they are already paired, how they tell their partners where they are and advertise the occupation of their territories.

Many owls call in duet, with one partner initiating and its mate completing the call. The calls of the sexes are often similar, and they are best distinguished by one (mostly the female) having a higher-pitched call than the other.

A Barn Owl with prey – the vlei rat is one of this owl's favourite prey items.

OWL PELLETS

Owls differ from diurnal raptors in the way they process their prey. A hawk or eagle that has caught a small mammal or bird usually plucks off and discards the fur or feathers before tearing up the flesh and swallowing it piece by piece. By contrast, an owl will swallow its prey unplucked and in one piece. Owls can't always do this, of course, and large items are dismembered to some extent, with individual pieces (always as large as possible) being swallowed in great gulps.

Diurnal raptors have a crop between the beak and the stomach which serves as a temporary storage area, and a hawk or eagle that has fed recently often has a conspicuous bulge in its breast. Owls, on the other hand, lack a crop and don't show visibly that they have just eaten. The food passes directly into their stomachs, where the digestible portions are processed. The indigestible parts (bones and fur) are compacted into a pellet which is regurgitated through the mouth six to 12 hours after the meal. Many species of birds regurgitate such pellets of indigestible material but in owls these pellets are often very distinctive. Easily found, they provide a wealth of information on the nature of the prey being caught.

ABOUT THIS BOOK

Seven groups of owls that are found widely in the world are represented in southern Africa. The eagle owls, which belong to the genus *Bubo*, are one such group, and three species in this genus (the Spotted Eagle Owl, Cape Eagle Owl and Giant Eagle Owl) are found in southern Africa. The eagle owls include the largest of the world's owls (*Bubo bubo*, weighing 2,5–3 kg), which occurs widely in the wilder parts of Europe and Asia. Africa's largest owl is the Giant Eagle Owl, in which the female (which is the larger sex in all owls) weighs 2–2,5 kg.

Looking rather like diminutive eagle owls are the tiny scops owls in the genus *Otus*, of which there are two species in the region (the Whitefaced Owl and the Scops Owl). The latter is southern Africa's smallest owl, weighing a mere 60-70 g and being about the size of a thrush.

The pygmy owls (belonging to the genus *Glaucidium*) are represented by two species (the Pearlspotted Owl and the Barred Owl) in the southern African region. Single species representing the genera *Asio* (the Marsh Owl), *Strix* (the

Wood Owl) and *Scotopelia* (Pel's Fishing Owl) are also found in the subregion.

The group to which the Barn Owl belongs is a separate family, known as the Tytonidae (or *Tyto* owls). This family includes the Barn Owl, the Grass Owl and a few other species not found in southern Africa. Their separation into a distinct family is based on their differently shaped face, their longer legs and other structural differences.

In this book, the southern African owls are grouped according to where they are likely to be found. Two species, the Barn Owl and the Spotted Eagle Owl, are often encountered in urban situations and, although they are also common in many other environments, because they are the main 'city' owls, they are dealt with in the chapter 'Beginners' Owls'.

The Marsh Owl and the Grass Owl live in grasslands, especially in vleis and marshy areas, and are dealt with in the chapter 'Owls in the Grass'.

The chapter 'Bushveld Owls' deals with the four species that are characteristic of savanna or 'bushveld' regions (the Scops Owl, the Whitefaced Owl, the Pearlspotted Owl and the Giant Eagle Owl).

The four species with the most limited ranges in southern Africa and the most specialised habitat requirements (the Wood Owl, the Barred Owl, the Cape Eagle Owl and Pel's Fishing Owl) are dealt with in 'Habitat Specialists'.

The concluding chapter, 'Hands-on Owling', discusses what you can do to protect and encourage owls, and also describes the photographic techniques we've used to capture owls on film.

An appendix with general statistical information about southern African owls is provided, and a glossary and 'Further Reading' list conclude the book.

CLASSIFICATION OF SOUTHERN AFRICAN OWLS

SUBORDER	FAMILY	GENUS	SPECIES	SUBSPECIES
STRIGI (all owls)	TYTONIDAE	*Tyto*	*alba* (Barn Owl)	
			capensis (African Grass Owl*)	
	STRIGIDAE	*Otus*	*senegalensis* (African Scops Owl*)	
			leucotis (Whitefaced Owl)	
		Bubo	*capensis* (Cape Eagle Owl)	*mackinderi* (Mackinder's Race)
				capensis (Cape Race)
			africanus (Spotted Eagle Owl)	
			lacteus (Giant Eagle Owl)	
		Strix	*woodfordii* (Wood Owl)	
		Glaucidium	*perlatum* (Pearlspotted Owl)	
			capense (African Barred Owl*)	*capense* (Coastal Race)
				ngamiense (Ngami Race)
		Asio	*capensis* (Marsh Owl)	
		Scotopelia	*peli* (Pel's Fishing Owl)	

* The addition of 'African' to the Grass Owl, Scops Owl and Barred Owl has been done to distinguish these species from other, unrelated, non-African species that also carry the names 'Grass Owl', 'Scops Owl' and 'Barred Owl'. In the southern African context of this book, however, no confusion should arise, so the word 'African' has been omitted.

FINDING OWLS

Without the appropriate tools and techniques, locating an owl in the landscape can be a bit like searching for a needle in a haystack. Learning about their calls, the habitats they favour, the sites they choose for daytime hideaways or for nests, their preference for familiar sites and their habit of 'whitewashing' below their perches, all make finding owls a lot easier.

Left: A Barn Owl breaks cover.

FINDING OWLS

A good start to owling is learning to 'read' the landscape. Different environments support different owl species, according to the presence of elements that are crucial to the individual species' survival. First, owls need an appropriate prey base if they are to occur in an area at all (for some owls this may be rodents, for others, insects, and so on). They also need hideaway sites where they can roost undisturbed during the day. In some species these hideaways fulfil their third need, too – that of suitable nesting sites. No two owl species have identical habitat requirements, and nowhere in southern Africa do the subregion's 12 owl species all occur side by side.

LISTENING FOR CALLS

Once you've identified places likely to be frequented by a particular species, you need to look for them at the best times – usually at dusk and dawn, when many owls are most active and vocal.

Walk quietly, and stop and listen frequently. Don't switch on your torch; this way, your eyes can become accustomed to the low-light conditions (it takes about 40 minutes for human eyes to become fully accustomed to darkness). Tune in to your own sense of hearing (which, as we've discussed, should be pretty good!) – among the host of other dusk sounds there may be owls calling, and it is usually the call that provides the first clue to an owl being in an area.

Different owl species have different calls – some hoot, some croak, some screech, some purr and some whistle. A knowledge of owls' calls is essential in order to identify, firstly, whether what you are hearing is, in fact, an owl and

Old farm buildings, a hay shed and open ground: all ingredients ideal for Barn Owl habitat. Large trees in the distance provide favourable habitat for Spotted Eagle Owls.

not, say, a frog or an insect, and secondly, what species of owl it is. Owl calls are best learnt by having them identified by someone who knows them, but they can also be learnt by listening to them on one of the commercially available bird tapes.

A Spotted Eagle Owl guarding its nearby nest where its mate incubates. Like most owls, it is most vocal before egg laying.

A knowledge of owl calls, as with any other bird calls, is not instantly gained but gradually built up as you are exposed to more and more species. Thus, the soft 'hu, hooo' hooting call of the Spotted Eagle Owl and the screech of the Barn Owl will quickly become part of a beginner's repertoire, whereas it may be years before an owler is exposed to the sombre call of Pel's Fishing Owl or the penetrating hoot of the Cape Eagle Owl.

In our experience, owls are most vocal in the one or two months preceding egg laying. Thus Spotted Eagle Owls, which lay most frequently in August and September, are most vocal in July and August, while Cape Eagle Owls, which breed earlier in the year, are vociferous in April and May. At other times of the year, the same birds may be virtually silent, hooting perhaps only once or twice during the course of a night.

CALL-PLAYBACK

Most owl species respond to playbacks of their calls. Incapable of recognising that the tape-recording of the call is not the real thing, any owl in the vicinity may come closer to investigate, and perhaps to challenge the bird it thinks is intruding on its territory.

If done minimally and sensitively, the use of call-playback to bring an owl closer and get a view of it should cause little or no disruption to the bird. However, because owls rely heavily on vocal communication, excessive playback can be highly disruptive. (It has recently been claimed that there are no owls breeding in Skukuza Camp in the Kruger National Park as a result of the excessive use of call-playback by visitors to the camp.) As with littering, the effect of it being done once may be minimal, whereas the cumulative effect of many people doing the same thing in the same place could be very stressful to the bird being targeted. For this reason, in all the national parks and many of the state parks in the USA, the use of call-playback is regarded as wildlife harassment and is prohibited.

A Wood Owl responding to playback of its call, a useful tool if you simply want a sighting of an owl.

The well-camouflaged Barred Owl blends into the leafy foliage.

When attempting to attract an owl using call-playback, play the tape softly at first; pause a while between calls to listen and watch for a response, and remember to cease playing the tape once the bird has come into view.

Owls' responses to playbacks vary according to both season and the amount of moonlight available; in general, owls are much less vocal on moonless nights than on moonlit nights. Different owls also respond differently: some may approach silently, view the proceedings and then withdraw; others may fly in and respond by calling vociferously; or they may circle about, calling. In our experience Barn Owls, Giant Eagle Owls and Pel's Fishing Owls are relatively indifferent or only mildly responsive to playbacks of their calls; all other southern African owls respond strongly.

Call-playback is useful if you simply want a sighting of the bird but, because it disrupts whatever activity the owls were engaged in beforehand, it spoils opportunities for observing the owls going about their normal business. There is much more to owls than a brief view of a highly charged bird responding to a taped call!

By listening to owls' calls without using call-playback, you may be able to establish whether it is a lone male calling or if a pair is involved. It could be that a lone male is attempting to attract a mate to a prospective nest site he has found, or that a pair are involved in courtship or are feeding young out of the nest. All these things can be discovered by giving time to listening to the owls and letting them do their own thing without interruption.

NIGHT DRIVES

Night drives in rural areas in an open vehicle with a spotlight often yield sightings of owls. Because they perch in prominent positions after dark, owls are often easy to pick up at these times. In contrast to nightjars and many of the crepuscular and nocturnal mammals, which are readily detected by their 'eye shine', owls' eyes do not reflect in torchlight, so it is their shape that is the clue to their presence.

A Pearlspotted Owl twists away from its nest after delivering its prey.

If you keep your distance, owls found in this way will not be disturbed by being spotlit and they may continue their normal activity. Train the light just off the bird so as not to dazzle it – while a spotlight will not damage an owl's eyes, it is likely to have the same effect as it would on human eyes, with readjustment to low-light conditions taking time.

SEARCHING BY DAY

Daytime searching for owls is made much easier if one has ascertained that a particular species is in the area. This, and a knowledge of their preferred habitat and, particularly, the sorts of place they choose as daytime hideaways or nest sites, will usually lead to their discovery. Mark the location of any owls found at night and search for them during the day to establish what they are up to.

Daytime searches are most likely to succeed if they focus on the object of finding the owls, rather than being a general nature ramble. For species that may lie up during the day in woodland, forest, rocky outcrops or shrubbery, you must be alert for signs of the bird's presence rather than the bird itself. (The grass-living owls are a special case; more will be said about

Above: Grass Owls take flight from their daytime roost. Centre: Grass Owl in flight.

them in a later chapter.) Firstly, be aware of any agitated calls being made in a particular spot by other small birds (for example bulbuls, white-eyes or sunbirds) as these could be mobbing an owl. On the other hand, they could also be mobbing a poisonous snake or one of a dozen other predators, so a cautious approach is needed to establish the cause for their concern.

Where undisturbed, owls often re-use the same hideaways day after day; once found, and provided they are not repeatedly chased from the site by too close an approach, the owls can be located there time after time. The location of these sites is often given away by the odd moulted feather, as well as by the faeces and regurgitated remains that accumulate on the ground below. A daytime search for an owl is thus often an eyes-to-the-ground scrutiny for white-wash, accumulations of soft, fluffy feathers, pieces of bone or skin, and pellets.

Well hidden, a pair of Spotted Eagle Owls at their daytime roost.

Barn Owl chicks wait in anticipation for their parent to deliver their meal.

The faeces of the little owls are barely noticeable. However, those of the larger owl species, like those of diurnal birds of prey, are voluminous white splashes which, when deposited on branches or rocks, are a dead giveaway. Bear in mind, though, that copious whitewashing on branches or on the ground is not always the work of an owl, and could originate from a hawk, vulture or eagle. You would need to find corroborating evidence by way of pellets or feathers to establish the identity of the 'whitewasher'.

Different owls produce different signs that may give away their presence. In a search for, say, a Pel's Fishing Owl, you would need to look carefully below all densely foliaged riverine trees for signs of whitewash, odd fish bones and, especially, uneaten fish heads and ginger-coloured

Left: A Marsh Owl, alert with its characteristic round face, and dark brown eyes.

Below: Signs which tell of the presence of a Pel's Fishing Owl – fish remains and a large ginger feather lying below the roost.

feathers; a Barn Owl search, on the other hand, would focus on concentrations of whitewash on the walls of old buildings, rock faces or the walls of old quarries, followed by a closer inspection below such sites for the characteristic smooth, round, grey pellets that distinguish this bird.

In the following chapters these and other clues will be looked at in more detail, species by species.

BEGINNERS' OWLS

THE SPOTTED EAGLE OWL AND THE
BARN OWL LIVE COMFORTABLY ALONG-
SIDE HUMAN BEINGS, AND, OF SOUTHERN
AFRICA'S TWELVE OWL SPECIES, ARE THE
ONES MOST LIKELY TO BE ENCOUNTERED
BY THE AVERAGE PERSON.

THEY THEREFORE FILL THE SLOT OF
'BEGINNERS' OWLS', AND PROVIDE A
WORTHY INTRODUCTION TO THE OWL
FAMILY SINCE THEY REPRESENT THE
WORLD'S TWO MAJOR OWL GROUPINGS.

Far left: Spotted Eagle Owls.
Left: Typical eagle owl profile.

BEGINNERS' OWLS

Precious few people have the luck of starting their owling adventures with a sighting of a Pel's Fishing Owl. For most mortals, their introduction to the world of owls is by a lesser bird – in all likelihood a Spotted Eagle Owl or Barn Owl, as these are the most widely distributed owls in southern Africa, and the most closely associated with manmade environments. As representatives of the two families that make up the owls of the world, they are good 'starter' owls.

Spotted Eagle Owls have ear tufts, which most people expect in an owl, and they hoot. Barn Owls have a ghostly, pale plumage and an ethereal-looking, heart-shaped face, and they utter the wailing screech that most people associate with dark nights and neglected cemeteries.

There is probably not a town in southern Africa that does not have Spotted Eagle Owls and/or Barns Owls in residence. Until the 1970s, Harare, Pieter-maritzburg and Grahamstown all had resident Barn Owls – Maritzburg's Barn Owls roosted in the town hall, Harare's in the post office and Grahamstown's in the cathedral. Barn Owls need open land for hunting, however, so they are no longer likely to be found in the centres of cities, and today occur mostly in the outer suburbs of such larger towns and cities.

Spotted Eagle Owls, on the other hand, are perfectly capable of surviving wherever there are gardens and parks, and in places where they can lie up during the day and nest undisturbed. Thus, Johannesburg, Cape Town, Pretoria and many other cities today still have resident populations of Spotted Eagle Owls in their centres. As an example of their urban flair, an owl which almost certainly belonged to this species was reported to have entered the bedroom of a Cape Town flat at night and, to the occupant's consternation, alighted on the bed!

SPOTTED EAGLE OWL

The Spotted Eagle Owl's success probably hinges on its general adapt-ability – it is unfussy about where it nests, what it eats and how it catches its prey. You can find Spotted Eagle Owls nesting and roosting in many places. Rocky koppies are always favoured, from the remote Tsodilo Hills in northwestern Botswana to Melville Koppies, a stone's throw from downtown Johannesburg.

The Spotted Eagle Owl often nests on the ground, favouring rocky outcrops.

The disused nests of birds of prey also provide nest sites for Spotted Eagle Owls.

They love copses of old trees, especially old eucalypts with bark-draped trunks and leafy canopies, lines of misshapen old willow trees, old pines with accumulations of needles caught in the branches, and thick-stemmed, pineapple-shaped palms. You can also find them in the walls of abandoned quarries, in erosion dongas where there is a recessed shelf, and in haystacks; and they sometimes nest on bare ground, simply creating a 'scrape' in which to lay their eggs.

Sites where Spotted Eagle Owls are able to nest successfully are often used year after year, and some spots have been in regular use for decades. Several pairs now nest in boxes put up especially for them in gardens, and a few nest in window boxes on houses and buildings where tolerant owners have let them.

SPOTTED EAGLE OWL

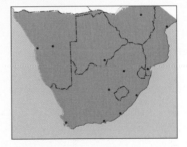

A large, grey-coloured owl, with prominent ear tufts and bright yellow eyes. Barred in front and blotched on the head, back and wings. (A rare morph, found in the dry regions of southern Africa, is brown in colour and has orange eyes.) Call, a mellow hooting. Length 450 mm.

Downy Spotted Eagle Owl chicks expectantly await food.

Ringing of selected birds has revealed that Spotted Eagle Owls remain paired for life, and that the same individuals reuse successful nest sites year after year. A particular female 'Spottie' – made famous by bird-man Geoff Lockwood, star of several television features – nested in Johannesburg's Delta Park for at least 21 years, the first 13 with one partner and the remainder with a second.

Suburban Spotted Eagle Owls accustomed to human company can become both confiding and aggressive, sitting tight instead of flying off when approached, but then attacking when approached too closely. Newspapers sometimes carry reports of people walking their dogs at dusk and being swooped on by 'ferocious' owls. Such 'attacks' are almost certainly by Spotted Eagle Owls, and are often precipitated by the person's having ventured too close to a nest or to chicks that have just left the nest. (Both authors have lost scalp blood to angry suburban Spotted Eagle Owls defending their nests!)

By contrast, rural owls tend to retreat and simply watch proceedings if their nests are approached, or, at worst, make angry, snapping sounds with their beaks. Very occasionally a nesting female will engage in a distraction display, feigning injury by hopping along the ground awkwardly and dragging a wing. Her partner usually joins the show by flying in and hooting loudly.

Nesting takes place in early summer, and in the months preceding this (May to August) Spotted Eagle Owls are most vocal. Theirs is a mellow hoot that can be deceptive where distance is concerned: the calling owl can be perched above your head, yet the sound will seem to be coming from far away. Although there are many variations on this, males usually utter a double hoot ('HU-hooo'), which is answered by the female with a softer, triple hoot ('ho-HU-hooo'). If you are close enough, you will see that the white throat of the calling bird becomes briefly conspicuous at each hoot.

During the two-and-a-half-month nesting period (incubation lasts about 31 days and the nestling period about 40 days), the owls centre their activity in the vicinity of the nest, but once the young are flying they range farther afield. The territorial area occupied by pairs is probably much affected by the availability of suitable nest sites; the closest recorded siting of adjacent nests of two distinct pairs was 500 metres apart.

In most cases, a clutch of two eggs is laid; less often, three are laid, and very occasionally four or five are laid. The chicks start wandering from the nest well before they can fly, and if the nest is situated on the ground, they vacate the nest scrape at about three weeks of age. Although ringing has revealed that adults are highly sedentary, young birds are more mobile and they may move a few dozen kilometres from their birthplace before establishing territories in which they then become sedentary. However, a remarkable recovery, recently reported, of a young bird ringed at Postmasburg in the Northern Cape and recovered eight months later at Saldanha, 695 kilometres away, may indicate that some juveniles disperse far more widely.

In natural habitats Spotted Eagle Owls tend to prey mainly on small to medium-sized rodents; in arid areas (such as the Namib and Karoo) gerbils and/or golden moles dominate their prey choice, while in bushveld and grassland areas the multimammate mouse is the single commonest recorded prey item. A study conducted in the Southern Cape region indicated that insects (for example grasshoppers, beetles, crickets and termites) made up the bulk of the owl's prey there. Everywhere, though, Spotted Eagle Owls have been shown to take a great variety of prey; in some areas birds up to the size of a francolin are commonly caught, while in others it may be geckos, bats or frogs that assume significance.

BARN OWL

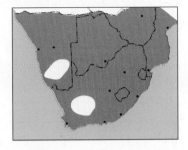

A medium-sized owl; white or buffy in colour, with warm orange and grey flecked with white on the wings and back, and with fine spots in front. Striking white, heart-shaped facial disc; black eyes and no ear tufts. Legs are long and white. Call, a tremulous screech. Length 320 mm.

The pellets cast by these owls are an important source of information regarding their diets, and the results of several thousand pellet contents have been reported on. The pellets of eagle owls lack the compact firmness of those cast by Barn Owls and Grass Owls, and they often break into fragments on the ground below a roost, making them less easy to find. Such pellets are always worth examining for the presence of bird rings; a Redfaced Mousebird, for example, which was ringed at Melville Koppies in January 1975, turned up in a Spotted Eagle Owl pellet there the following October.

Prey is secured in various ways. When hunting, Spotted Eagle Owls change perches frequently, scanning the ground below for movement. In towns, telephone poles are often used for this, and along country roads, fence posts. Spotted Eagle Owls have also been reported perching on floodlights and dropping to the ground to catch insects attracted to the light. Dignity is often forsaken in such activity, and a Spotted Eagle Owl in hot pursuit on foot after a fleeing scarab beetle is a pretty comical sight! These owls often alight on roads at night, probably attracted to insects crossing, and as a result many are killed by passing vehicles. Peter Steyn reports, in his book on birds of prey (see 'Further Reading', page 84), no fewer than 26 dead Spotted Eagle Owls were counted along a 200-kilometre stretch of road in Namibia.

Most Spotted Eagle Owls are predominantly

Above: Spotted Eagle Owl with prey.
Bottom left: Young Barn Owls peeping from their willow tree nest hole.

grey, finely barred on their underparts, and have bright yellow eyes. A few deviate from this plumage by having either pale, sandy plumage or rufous coloration and orange eyes. These latter birds are easily mistaken for Cape Eagle Owls and, since there are places where the two species occur side by side, care in their identification needs to be exercised. One telling difference between the two is that Cape Eagle Owls have a spangle of warm, orange-brown feathers on their neck and chest, and their underparts are boldly rather than finely barred.

BARN OWL

Never would a Barn Owl be mistaken for a 'Spottie': the two are chalk and cheese. The world's most numerous owl species, Barn Owls have a vast range – across five continents, as well as on many offshore islands – and occur in dozens of forms, with as many as 38 different races having been described.

The African race, *Tyto alba affinis*, is one of the larger Barn Owl races and has a wide range on the continent, being plentiful in many parts of southern

ANALYSING OWL PELLETS

Even the most casual examination of an owl's pellet will reveal that it contains bits and pieces of its last meal – fur, pieces of bone, feathers, fish scales, grasshopper legs, bird's beaks or the scales of a lizard, depending on the kind of owl involved. All that is needed to analyse the contents of the pellet is some resourcefulness and forensic aptitude in quantifying and identifying the fragments involved.

Owl pellets are not unpleasant to work with, and they are easy to collect and keep until they can be analysed. First, you should establish with certainty what species of owl is producing the pellets or the information won't have much relevance. Secondly, all batches of pellets should be labelled (with the species, locality and date) and kept in a closed bag with naphthalene balls to prevent moth attack.

The first step in the analysis is to soak the pellets in water (to which a drop of disinfectant could be added) then, one by one, tease them apart using tweezers. Record the contents of each pellet separately. Sort similar items into piles – bones in one pile, insect remains in another, and so on. Mammal fur is usually discarded since its identification requires relatively sophisticated microscopic techniques.

The presence of insect body parts, scales, etc, is usually recorded only qualitatively (for example, 'pellet contained remains of dung beetles and grasshoppers, and lizard

Characteristic Barn Owl pellets (with butterfly for scale).

The pellets and chalky white faeces of a Cape Eagle Owl.

scales'). The remains of birds (especially their skulls and beaks) and small mammals (skulls and lower jaws) can be more precisely quantified by counting the number of skulls/beaks/jaws of each species found in each pellet. In the case of small mammals, the identification of these is made possible by looking for species-specific features on the skulls and teeth, and systematically working these through a key (Coetzee's identification key and De Graaff's rodent book describing skull morphology will be helpful for this; see 'Further Reading' on page 84). Look for clues such as whether the front incisors are grooved or ungrooved, and the molars laminated or unlaminated, and whether there are three or five roots in the third molar?

Once the identification of the 20–30 small mammal species that commonly occur in owl pellets is mastered, their quantification in pellets becomes easier.

A Barn Owl pair at a regular perch site; the female (left) is darker than the male.

Africa. Males and females are very similar in size and colour; females may be more heavily spotted in front, and weigh more than males. They live in pairs, although single birds may also be found.

Barn Owls call a great deal, even on the darkest nights. Their shrill, rather eerie screech – a sound that must strike terror into the hearts of mice, as it does some men! – is given by both sexes, both in flight and while perched.

Barn Owls are strictly nocturnal, emerging from their daytime hideaways at dusk and returning to them at first

Above: A Barn Owl in flight.

moles), and evidence of this abounds from many parts of southern Africa; at least 20 000 prey items identified in pellets have been reported on in various publications. In all of these, small mammals comprised 80 to 95 percent of the recorded prey. In the wetter regions (the savanna and grassland biomes) the dominant prey species is the multi-mammate mouse (usually followed by the vlei rat and/or pouched mouse), whereas in the more arid regions (the Karoo, Kalahari and Namib) one or other of the gerbil species dominates the prey list.

Barn Owl pellets sometimes hold as much interest for non-owlers as they do for owlers. For example, the type specimen (that is, the first specimen known to science) of the Namib Desert's Grant's golden mole came from a Barn Owl pellet, and ornithologist Carl Vernon discovered the first Zimbabwe specimens of the rare Rudd's mouse in Barn Owl pellets which he collected from a hollow tree on the Lundi River.

light. (Much has been written about what Barn Owls do at night, and about their remarkable ability to catch mice in total darkness, and some of this has been described in the Introduction, on page 9.) They specialise in hunting small, nocturnal mammals (rodents, shrews and

Barn Owls during a 'boom' year: parent (right) and young (left) of different ages.

BREEDING: BOOM OR BUST

What is most fascinating to us about Barn Owls is their 'boom or bust' breeding strategy. Much has been written about it, and we have witnessed it for ourselves several times. The fact that Barn Owls are creatures of habit, roosting and nesting at the same spot for years on end, makes it easy to monitor them and their breeding activity. We keep tabs on the nesting pairs in our neighbourhoods, RE in the farmlands around Potchefstroom and WT around Nylsvley. In some years only a few of the pairs breed and their clutches are small; in other years heaps of them are to be found nesting and many more eggs per clutch are laid. The year 1994 was just such a 'boom' year, followed by a 'bust' year in 1995. At Potchefstroom an average of about four or five active nests are usually found per annum; 1994 was, in fact, a 'megaboom' year, with 24 active nests being found. In 'average' years Barn Owls laid an average of six eggs per clutch; in 1994 the average increased to nearly nine, with two pairs laying clutches of 18 and 19 eggs. By contrast, in 1995 not a single one of the Potchefstroom pairs was found nesting.

At Nylsvley, the Tarbotons have shared their home with Barn Owls since 1991,

when a nest box was installed under the house's eaves. The box was instantly occupied (the following night!) and the owls have been there ever since. They bred once in 1991, rearing four young; not at all in 1992; twice in 1993, rearing broods of four and three young; once in the megaboom year of 1994, laying 16 eggs from which 12 young were reared; not at all in 1995; and twice in 1996, rearing four young. In the six consecutive years the breeding performance of this pair levelled out to a clutch a year (six clutches, averaging 6,8 eggs per clutch), with 4,5 young per annum being reared. Behind the average figures is the real story of the Barn Owl's boom-or-bust approach to reproduction.

If situated appropriately, nest boxes hold a magnetic attraction for Barn Owls, and we have seen them successfully installed against the outside walls of houses and water tanks, on the inside and outside of barns, silos and other farm buildings, and against the trunks of trees.

In the absence of nest boxes, Barn Owls look for dark holes in which to nest.

Long legs thrown forward, a Barn Owl alights at a nest box.

Disused Hamerkop nests are a great favourite, and, in a study of nesting Barn Owls made by West African ornithologist RT Wilson in Mali, every single one of the 178 Barn Owl nests examined was in a Hamerkop nest! In southern Africa the proportion is not as high as this, but even in our region Hamerkops provide homes for a significant number of Barn Owls. In addition to the sites mentioned, we have found nests in holes in trees (baobabs are a favourite), in holes in cliffs and quarries, in the ceilings and lofts of houses, in church towers, pigeon cotes, mine shafts, farm machinery and bales of lucerne, in an abandoned army bunker, in chimneys and, once, in a fireplace. In boom years adjacent pairs may nest as close as 50 metres to one another.

Successful Barn Owl nest sites are dark and give cover to the bird/s during the daylight hours. Barn Owls do not like light – and perhaps with good reason, as one, inadvertently flushed by one of us from its hideaway on a cliff face during the day, was very quickly dispatched by a Lanner Falcon!

Barn Owls may nest at any time of the year, and in particularly suitable years the female may commence laying a second clutch while the last young of the previous brood are still in the nest. Although highly variable, the highest incidence of egg laying occurs in southern Africa during the months of March and April, which coincides with that time of the year when rodent numbers are at their highest levels. Multimammate mice, the main prey over much of the

Above: A rodent's tail is gulped down by a Barn Owl chick. Bottom: Barn Owl reveals white underparts.

owl's range, undergo periodic population irruptions, and it is presumably in these times that the owls breed so prolifically. The number of chicks that they rear per clutch is, however, extremely variable, and probably correlates directly with the amount of food that the parents are capable of catching and bringing to the nest. (At times we have seen up to 30 uneaten mice lying amid a brood of chicks in a nest.)

Successful years probably result in a large increment of new owls being added to the population. Some starve, some probably drown, and many die on roads; those that survive probably disperse widely across the subcontinent before they reach maturity, find partners and breed. A glimpse into this post-fledging world of the Barn Owl is provided by a ringing recovery, the farthest-flung one so far obtained for a Barn Owl: the bird was ringed as a nestling in the Kalahari Gemsbok National Park's Nossob Camp and was recovered five years later, drowned in a water tank, 579 kilometres away, near Rustenburg.

OWLS IN THE GRASS

As their names clearly imply, the Grass Owl and the Marsh Owl are two species that one would expect to find living on the ground. These are the most terrestrial-living of the subcontinent's owls, and spend most of their non-flying hours hidden from view in rank grass or in the marshy vegetation associated with wetlands.

Far left: Marsh Owl on roadside perch.
Left: Grass Owl chick.

OWLS IN THE GRASS

MARSH AND GRASS OWLS

Grasslands may seem an unlikely biome to harbour owls, yet two species, the Marsh Owl and Grass Owl, are entirely restricted to such habitats. Both these species lie up in long grass during the day, and both rest and nest on the ground much like a game bird. The areas favoured by both are marshy bottom-lands – probably because these sites offer the best cover – but neither species is entirely confined to wet situations; at times, birds of both species may be found kilometres from the nearest water. In suitable areas Grass Owls and Marsh Owls may occur side by side, and they have even been found nesting within 250 metres of each other.

Despite sharing the same habitat and being superficially alike, the two species are only distantly related. Grass Owls are *Tyto* owls (family Tytonidae), and their closest kinship is with the Barn Owl, to which they bear a close resemblance. Marsh Owls are members of the other owl family, the Strigidae; they belong to the genus *Asio*, which includes the northern hemisphere's ground-living Short-eared Owl – with which the Marsh Owl shares many features.

Grass Owls and Marsh Owls are among the most commonly misidentified of all the southern African owls, and reports abound in which the one has been mistaken for the other. If you look at the illustrations of the two, such confusion is hard to understand. They differ in size; one has a white front, the other a dark front; and one has a pale, heart-shaped face, the other a brown face.

So, why the confusion? Usually these birds are sighted when the owl is flushed from long grass: it planes away and drops back into the grass, out of sight, giving a brief rear view of a brown-winged, brown-backed, 'headless' bird. If it were to bank and circle, giving a front view before disappearing, its identity would be obvious. This seldom happens, however, especially in the case of the Grass Owl.

Dark brown upperparts distinguish this alighting bird as a Grass Owl.

We have found that the best field character to look for is whether or not there is a pale ginger panel in the outer wing (on the top surface, at the base of the primaries). If there is, the bird is a Marsh Owl. If the entire length of the upperwing appears uniformly brown, the bird is a Grass Owl. It needs only the briefest view to ascertain this, but you need to know exactly what to look for.

SPOT THE DIFFERENCE

Although the two species often live in the same areas, they are quite different birds. Firstly, Marsh Owls are far commoner than Grass Owls, outnumbering them, on average, by nine to one. Their overall range is much greater, extending into even the driest parts of Namibia; they are likely to occur in a wider range of grassland habitats; and they invariably occur in greater numbers than Grass Owls, even where both species occur together in the same area.

Grass Owls are restricted to the eastern half of southern Africa, where the rainfall is highest; they have not, for example, been recorded in Namibia, and their greatest concentration seems to lie in the regions receiving 700–800 mm of rain annually, especially in the highveld grasslands. Their affinity for higher-rainfall areas may have to do with their preference for long grass and good grass cover. Marsh Owls do occur in such vegetation but they also tolerate much sparser cover.

Both species are nomadic, and probably move from area to area in response to changing conditions. In the case of the Marsh Owl this nomadism is much more apparent since they often roost in loose aggregations. Twenty to 40 (and occasionally up to 75) birds can be flushed from the same general area; and such flocks can be there one day and gone the next. This flocking can occur at any time of the year but is most prevalent during midsummer, when little or no breeding occurs.

Grass Owls never flock. They are normally encountered singly or in pairs, but sometimes after the breeding season a pair and their offspring will remain together for a time in loose association.

GRASS OWL

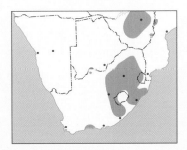

A medium-sized owl; white or buffy in colour. Pale with fine spots in front, and dark brown with white spots on the wings and back. Striking white, heart-shaped facial disc; small, black eyes and pale bill; no ear tufts. Legs are long and white, and tail white with dark centre. Call, a rapid frog-like series of clicks in flight. Length 360 mm.

The third noticeable difference between Grass Owls and Marsh Owls has to do with their relative activity during daylight hours. Grass Owls are among the most nocturnal of the owls – they don't normally leave their roosts to hunt until at least half an hour after sunset and they are seldom seen in daylight hours except when they have been flushed from a roost. We have occasionally witnessed Grass Owls hunting in daylight, but this has usually been after they have been disturbed at their roost by a veld fire and have taken the opportunity to hunt rodents escaping the flames.

Marsh Owls, on the other hand, are probably our least nocturnal owls, and hunting birds are often seen on the wing before sunset and

Grass Owl on silent wings.

after sunrise, especially in autumn and winter. If you do ever see a 'Grass Owl' out and about before dark, check its identity carefully.

Both species prey mainly on small rodents and shrews which they catch in the grass. Grass Owls prey almost exclusively on these small mammals and they particularly favour vlei rats, whereas Marsh Owls include insects (grasshoppers and beetles especially) and a variety of non-rodent prey, such as roosting birds, ducklings and lizards, in their diet.

These differences are readily detectable by examining the pellets of the two species. Grass Owls' pellets, which are firm and strongly compacted, usually contain only the fur and bones of rodents or shrews. Marsh Owl pellets almost invariably contain insect fragments in

A Grass Owl male arrives at its nest, well hidden in long grass, with prey for its mate.

addition to the remains of small mammals and perhaps other taxa; as a result, they lack the cohesion of Grass Owl pellets and break up easily.

Grass Owls and Marsh Owls both breed mainly at the end of summer (March to May). While at other times of the year roosting birds may frequently change the location of where they lie up during the day, during the breeding season they keep to one spot, and it is here that the eggs are eventually laid. Both species lay very rounded, similarly sized, white eggs, up to five in a clutch.

MARSH OWL

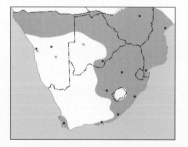

A medium-sized owl; uniform dull brown in colour, barred with rufous in the wings. Facial disc off-white with dark smudges around the eyes; eyes are dark brown, ear tufts are small but often not visible. Call a raspy croak. Length 360 mm.

Unlike their eggs, the nests of the two species are usually distinguishable. Marsh Owls lay their eggs on a saucer-like bed of dry grass, about 300 mm in diameter, which is screened from above by a canopy of growing grass. Grass Owls make a tunnel in the grass, or a series of linking tunnels which can extend over one or two metres, roofed with bent-over long grass, and they lay their eggs at the end of one of these tunnels on a flimsy grass floor.

A Marsh Owl feeding its chick; its nest is a saucer-like bed of dry grass.

In both species, the female does the incubation, during which time she is fed by her mate. When incubating, the female sits tight; if approached by an observer, she'll fly off only at the last moment. Grass Owls usually fly directly away and disappear from view, whereas nesting Marsh Owls are often more demonstrative, circling back, calling, and sometimes engaging in an elaborate injury-feigning display, landing nearby and flopping in the grass with one or both wings extended, uttering a distressing squealing noise. Such behaviour is a sure sign of a nest or chicks in the vicinity.

A further difference between the species relates to the age at which the chicks

Typical threat display, shared by many owl species, of a captive Marsh Owl.

disperse. Grass Owl chicks remain as a brood in the nest until close to fledging, whereas Marsh Owl chicks wander from the nest long before they can fly, with the result that the unfledged brood may be scattered widely in the vicinity of the nest.

The calls of the two species are quite different. Marsh Owls utter a rasping croak, sounding like a piece of material being torn. Grass Owls, long described as 'silent owls', give a repeated, rhythmic, high-pitched clicking that rises and falls in intensity and increases in tempo when two birds approach each other or when prey is brought to the nest. This we discovered when RE traced a sound he'd often heard after dark to a Grass Owl. We now know that Grass Owls call a lot while flying about, especially before and during the breeding season.

HUNTING TECHNIQUES

Because of their diurnal habits and the open nature of the terrain they frequent, Marsh Owls are among the easiest of owls to locate and watch. In autumn and winter one quartering back and forth over open grassland in the late afternoon or early morning is a common sight. This quartering is one of their hunting techniques: they fly in long, meandering lines at near-stalling speed about a metre above the ground, looking this way and that, and landing occasionally before taking off again and resuming the systematic search for prey. Every now and then the owl hovers briefly, or does a half somersault and drops down into the grass, sometimes emerging with prey, sometimes coming up without it. Prey items are often cached, usually on the ground, in an open spot, and the hunt resumed. It is thought that these owls cache some of their prey in order not to waste good hunting time, returning only later to eat it.

Quartering Marsh Owls are seldom seen in summer, suggesting that all necessary hunting during this season can be accomplished in darkness, whereas in winter diurnal hunting may be necessary to make ends meet. The food demands of a brood of chicks may necessitate the longer hunting hours during the early winter months, hence the more frequent sighting of these birds at this time.

Opportunities to observe Marsh Owls hunting after dark are much less forthcoming, although the birds are commonly encountered in the dark standing on the ground, often in old lands, on road verges and in other bare areas, and they may be hunting insects when doing this.

Out hunting in the late afternoon, a Marsh Owl slowly quarters the ground.

A Marsh Owl brood.

A researcher studying Blackfooted Cats near Kimberley (see 'Further Reading', page 84) reported the interesting observation that a Marsh Owl sometimes joined the cat that was being watched late at night, hovering a few metres above it for half an hour or more. On at least one occasion the owl caught a lark that the cat had disturbed and flushed into the air.

In contrast to Marsh Owl hunting behaviour, that of Grass Owls is little studied. The nocturnal nature of Grass Owls has prevented any extensive observations of their hunting activity. We have sat in the dark beside a marsh and heard the steady clicking note of a flying Grass Owl as it coursed up and down the vlei, never seeing the bird but able to track it by its steady calling. We presume such birds are hunting, but why they should call while doing so is uncertain. Research to determine whether this calling may have some echolocation function is underway. If it has, it will be the first owl species in which this technique, so well developed in bats, is known.

OWLS AT RISK

The question often asked about the Marsh and Grass owls is, why is the one a common bird and the other relatively rare? (The Grass Owl is listed in the most recent revision of the South African Bird Red Data Book, which is a list of those species that are at risk and require concentrated attention.) Although the differences between the two species have been highlighted here, the fact is that both share a liking for the same habitat and the same prey.

Our experience with these species suggests that Grass Owls are more sensitive to a deterioration in grass cover than are Marsh Owls. In years of good rainfall we find Grass Owls present and nesting in many of the vleis that we visit. During drought years, however, vleis come under increasingly severe grazing pressure and many dry up, and the grass cover is reduced or even eliminated. Grass Owls simply disappear from many of these sites, and in the places where they remain, they don't attempt to breed.

An unusual sight: a Marsh Owl showing its normally 'hidden' ear tufts.

By contrast, Marsh Owls will often remain in severely impacted areas, and they sometimes even nest successfully in heavily grazed and trampled sites. Perhaps because of their smaller size (Marsh Owls weigh about 320 g, Grass Owls about 420 g), Marsh Owls can avoid predators more effectively in sparser cover than can Grass Owls; furthermore, their strategy of early chick dispersal from the nest may be more advantageous than that of the Grass Owl in such conditions.

The less specialised diet and hunting methods of Marsh Owls may also contribute to their greater abundance. While preying mainly on small mammals, their greater ability to take beetles, birds, reptiles and amphibians may enhance their ability to survive in poor conditions.

The conservation of these two grass-living owls centres on maintaining sufficient habitat for them. Both species occur mainly in vleis where the longer grass habitat they favour is best developed.

In communal grazing lands where a 'right of common' approach to land use is adhered to, severe overgrazing is frequently the result, and there are big gaps in the Grass Owl and Marsh Owl distributions around these areas as a result of the demise here of their preferred habitats.

Severe overgrazing adversely affects both species, but especially the Grass Owl. Most of southern Africa's Grass Owl populations occur in well-managed, pastoral farming areas where the vleis are spared severe overgrazing.

Because they breed mainly in autumn and winter, the nests of the Grass Owl and the Marsh Owl are vulnerable to destruction by fire, and there are frequent reports of nests being lost in this way. The critical period is the owls' breeding season, March to May, and landowners could enhance the cause of these owls if they prevented burning during this period.

Above: A Grass Owl in its typical habitat of rank grass and sedges. Top: When flushed, Marsh Owls show themselves only briefly, then drop back into the grass, out of sight.

BUSHVELD OWLS

The bushveld regions support southern Africa's greatest diversity of owls. Some of these species also occur in cities, villages and forested areas elsewhere. But there are four that are restricted to the bushveld only. After sunset these species – the Scops Owl, Pearlspotted Owl, Giant Eagle Owl and Whitefaced Owl – bring life to the bushveld nights.

Left: The 'famous' Nossob camp Whitefaced Owl.
Below: A young Giant Eagle Owl.

BUSHVELD OWLS

It is dusk, a special time in the bushveld when the day's heat finally dissipates and the changeover from daytime activity to nightlife gets underway. The last notes of the scrub robins are heard; a jackal howls in the distance; a drongo calls a few shrill notes. The drongo's next calls include some separate, piercing whistles, followed by a series of whistles. But is it a drongo imitating, or has a Pearlspotted Owl started calling? A few minutes later we know it is a 'Pearlie': it starts with its wind-up call this time, and follows with a full-blown crescendo of 'tiu-tiu-tiu-tiu-tiu-tiu-tiu' notes that grow to a tremendous volume – especially for such a slip of a bird. It calls on intermittently, joined now and again by a second bird with a higher-pitched call.

From the western sky, still glowing pink, the next performer enters. At first just a few grunting notes are heard: 'uh, uhu, uh, uh'. There is a pause, a few more grunts, then the first bird's notes are joined by a deeper-pitched double grunt. Giant Eagle Owls! They call a while, then fall silent.

Other night sounds are now joining in. A distant Scops Owl begins calling, its ventriloquial, trilling 'prrrup' more insect-like than bird-like. Shortly another bird responds, and soon we can hear 'Scopsies' calling from several directions. Now that they've started, they'll be calling for the rest of the night.

Well into the evening the fourth of the bushveld owls joins in. At first we hear only a simple 'whooo', but with successive notes we begin to pick up the whole refrain, a rapid, stuttering 'who-who-who-who-WHOOO', the last note accented. It is a Whitefaced Owl. It calls for perhaps ten minutes then falls silent, leaving the stage clear for the persistent Scops Owls.

WHERE ARE THEY FOUND?

The bushveld owls are so grouped because they share very similar ranges. These are the African continent's four savanna-belt owls, whose ranges extend through from West to East Africa and down to southern Africa, entering the subcontinent in Namibia and Botswana, the Northern Cape, Northern and North-West provinces of South Africa, and Mozambique. Their ranges end when they come up against the karoo biome and the grasslands of South Africa.

A Pearlspotted Owl has difficulty getting itself and its prey into its nest.

SCOPS OWL

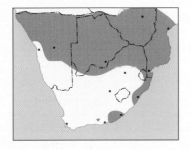

A tiny grey-coloured owl, streaked with grey, black and brown. (A rare morph is rufous-coloured.) Ear tufts are elongated and stand erect when the bird roosts in concealed positions during the day; eyes are bright yellow. Call a frog-like 'prrup'. Length 170 mm.

Some species penetrate farther south than others. The Pearlspotted Owl, for example, does not extend farther south than northeastern KwaZulu-Natal, whereas Scops Owls follow islands of savanna biome southwards down the eastern edge of the subcontinent into the Eastern Cape.

Depending on whether their habitat needs are met in the area, other owl species join the foursome. If there is open ground and a few old buildings or Hamerkop nests, Barn Owls can be expected; a rocky koppie and Spotted Eagle Owls will be there; a large marshy area and the chances are good for Marsh Owls and perhaps Grass Owls; in the warm lowveld country, Barred Owls may put in an appearance; and where slow-flowing, forest-lined rivers traverse the low country, Wood Owls and Pel's Fishing Owls will be present. The owl complement in savanna areas therefore varies according to where you are and what habitats occur together. The first seven owls listed are common at Nylsvley (where WT lives), and represent the owl community you can expect to find in much of the subcontinent's savanna regions.

SCOPS OWL

One would expect the smallest of the bushveld owls, the Scops Owl, to be the most numerous in the bushveld, as size and spatial requirements often correlate. Though this is the case in many areas (one usually hears more Scops Owls calling than any other owl) they are inexplicably rare in, or even absent from, large tracts of bushveld. They seem to favour areas with tall, scattered trees, between which is plenty of bare ground; if the trees are gnarled with dead branches, so much the better. Mopane woodland is favoured above all other habitats.

A Scops Owl pair at their nest hole in an old dead tree stump.

Being strictly nocturnal, Scops Owls are not easy to study, so relatively little is known about them. When they are not calling Scops Owls are extremely difficult to detect, and most people's sole experience of the birds is through calling them up with a tape at night, and seeing them glare down at the light from a high branch. With luck, you might spot or be shown a 'Scopsie' roosting during the day, pressed against a tree trunk, feathers drawn in, ear tufts erect and eyes closed to slits. Undisturbed, such birds usually use the same spot day after day; they are often found in the Kruger National Park's northern camps and their whereabouts is usually known to the camp attendants.

Scops Owls seem to prey primarily on small animals which they hunt from a low perch and pick up off the ground. We have recorded cockroaches, mole crickets, mantises, lizards, worms, solifuges, spiders, moths and, especially, *Noctuid* moth larvae being brought to a nest to feed chicks.

Although there are records of Scops Owls using artificial boxes as nests, they usually breed in natural holes in trees, favouring holes 200–500 mm deep and with a vertical entrance. Such holes can be invisible from below, and can be difficult to locate. Compounding this is the lack of clues provided by the nesting birds: while the female is incubating, the male is invisible to the world, pressed against a branch some distance away.

Two to four eggs are laid, and the incubation, by the female only, lasts 25 days, during which time she is fed by the male. The female is hard to budge from the nest, covering it so well (with her head tucked in and presenting a view of her back only) that when the hole is inspected, she looks just like the base of the hole.

Early in the nestling period the male continues to feed the female and provision the chicks, but later she joins in feeding the brood. The feeding tempo can be high (in seven hours one night RE recorded 66 feeding visits to a brood of seven-day-old chicks). Feeding continues through the night until dawn, when the parents retire.

PEARLSPOTTED OWL

In contrast to the Scops Owl's strictly nocturnal lifestyle is the capacity of the Pearlspotted Owl to keep going round the clock. Nesting Pearlspotted Owls are as likely to bring food to their nests at midday as at midnight, and at the on-set of the breeding season, when they are vocally most active, their calling continues as much by day as after dark. The call is easily imitated, and whistling like a Pearlspotted Owl is an effective way of attracting small bushveld birds, which fly in to mob the supposed predator.

Because of their diurnal habits Pearl-spotted Owls are probably the best known of the bushveld owls. About the size of a Crested Barbet, they weigh about 75 g and are stockily built, with a big head, squat body and a relatively long, very expressive tail. When agitated, they switch their tails jerkily from side to side. 'Pearlies' never have the sleepy look of many nocturnal owls in daytime: in their company, you are invariably fixed with a fierce, penetrating stare, punctuated by jerky head movements as the bird looks briefly left or right. This is one owl that can rotate its head in a complete circle – at one moment it may be regarding you over its left shoulder, the next over its right.

Although not greatly different in size, Pearlspotted Owls are far more rapacious than Scops Owls and frequently prey on other birds. Mousebirds, finches, weavers, warblers and robins – even a large nestling Laughing Dove, weighing substantially more than the owl – have been recorded in their diet. Birds do not, however, form their main prey, which consists rather of smaller items like beetles, solifuges, termite alates, frogs, lizards and rodents.

Nesting occurs during the early months of summer, when such prey items are on the increase, and July and August are the months when Pearlspotted Owls are most vocal, each pair entrenching its place in the region.

In suitable areas of habitat in the Nylsvley area the density of these owls is about one pair per 100 hectares. Pairs live all year round in the same territories, and during the breeding season (which normally lasts about two-and-a-half months) activity is focused on the nest site. This is invariably a hole in a tree, usually one excavated by a woodpecker or Crested Barbet. Such holes, often reused each year by the owls, may be occupied outside of the owls' breeding season by other hole-nesters such as kingfishers, hoopoes and starlings.

Finding 'Pearlies' and their nests is not difficult. Their calling makes them easy to home in on, and a scout around the area

PEARLSPOTTED OWL

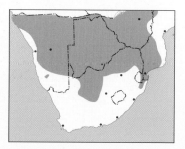

A tiny owl; white in front with elongated brown streaks; brown on the head, wings and back with white spots and streaks. Lacks ear tufts. Eyes bright yellow. Call, a series of piercing whistled notes rising in crescendo. Length 180 mm.

A Pearlspotted Owl flicks its long tail agitatedly during its early morning hunt.

looking for a woodpecker hole in a suitable tree is usually quickly rewarded. A sure sign of imminent breeding is a particular call note given by the female in the weeks preceding egg-laying. At this time of the year she relies on the male to feed her and remains in the vicinity of the nest, uttering a soft 'tu-weep' every now and then, presumably urging him to bring more food. The pair often also calls in duet at this time of the year, the male initiating the call with lower-pitched notes, after a while joined by the female with higher-pitched notes.

This huge size difference is very noticeable if a pair is seen together.

Both sexes utter a series of grunting hoots, from two or three to 15 or more in a sequence, which descend the scale then rise. These gruff notes, sometimes given by a single bird, sometimes by a pair calling in tandem, carry surprisingly well, and on a clear, windless night may be heard several kilometres away.

In areas of prime habitat (parkland or open bushveld with tall trees and suitable nest sites) Giant Eagle Owls sometimes occur at a density of about one pair per 7 000 hectares – an area that would support seventy times as many Pearlspotted Owls. Giant Eagle Owls are seen frequently in the Kalahari Gemsbok National Park; here, a ranger in the park, Kotie Herholdt, made a study of these birds and found that pairs were spaced at an average interval of 9,5 kilometres along the Auob River, and at intervals of 22 kilometres along the Nossob, where available nest sites appeared to be more widely spaced.

Giant Eagle Owls can be found during the day by searching for them in the leafy foliage of tall trees in areas where they

Above right: Pearlspotted Owl with prey.

GIANT EAGLE OWL

Sharing the bushveld habitat with these, the smallest of the African continent's owls, is Africa's largest owl, the Giant Eagle Owl. In this species, females are much larger than males (weighing, respectively, about 2,6 kg and 1,7 kg).

GIANT EAGLE OWL

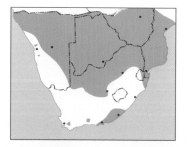

A very large, grey-coloured owl; darker on the back than front, finely vermiculated below. Black rim to the facial disc, with black eyes and pink eyelids. Has prominent ear tufts. Call, a series of deep grunts. Length 620 mm.

have been heard calling at night. Strictly nocturnal birds, they sit quietly during the day, the two birds of a pair often in close proximity. Whitewashing on the ground and the presence of prey remains are good clues to look for, since the birds often use the same roosting spots for extended periods, and their faeces and pellets accumulate on the ground. You will do them a grave disservice if you flush them from their cover, however, as the chances are they will be set upon by other birds, such as crows, kites or drongos, and their day's peace will be destroyed.

Hidden in the foliage of a riverine tree, a Giant Eagle Owl at its daytime roost.

During their protracted (four-and-a-half- to five-month) breeding season, the pair remains largely in the vicinity of the nest; to locate the birds, carefully scan any large stick nest in a tree for the telltale presence of 'ears' protruding from the top – a sign of a parent owl on its nest. In the Kalahari, Giant Eagle Owls love to use the tops of Sociable Weaver nests for this purpose; elsewhere, their choice is the old nest of any eagle or other large bird of prey (the list of species whose nests have recorded being used runs to a dozen or more). In a sample of about 50 Giant Eagle Owl nests we have examined, nearly half had originally been Wahlberg's Eagle nests, while several owl pairs had selected the tops of Hamerkop nests (on two occasions while the Hamer-kops were themselves nesting inside!).

Giant Eagle Owls breed in midwinter, laying their clutch of two large, round, white eggs in June, July or August. The chicks hatch after an incubation period of about 38 days, but rarely is more than one chick reared from the clutch. The surviving chick leaves the nest at about two months old, usually well before it can fly.

Prey remains and pellets accumulate on and near the nest, and you can learn a great deal about the pair's diet by inspecting these. Your first conclusion when looking through these will probably be that the owls are taking a huge variety of prey, in terms of both the size and type of animal taken. In the Nylsvley district, hedgehogs are clear favourites (comprising 44 out of 70 prey items we have recorded), and they are especially easily detected, as the

thorny skins which the owls peel off before eating them accumulate on the ground below a favourite perch. A great variety of birds is taken, including other owls (especially Barn Owls), game birds, ducks, crows, dikkops and nestling herons; other

A Giant Eagle Owl crouched low on its nest, originally built by a Wahlberg's Eagle.

WHITEFACED OWL

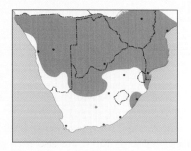

A fairly small owl with pale grey upperparts and white underparts; plumage finely streaked with black. Has a conspicuous white facial disc, rimmed with black; prominent ear tufts and bright orange eyes. Call, a ripple of stuttering hoots; sounds like a single hoot from a distance. Length 250 mm.

Breeding atop a Sociable Weaver's nest, a Giant Eagle Owl feeds its single chick.

items include hares, mongooses, polecats, small rodents, frogs, beetles and crickets. If you added up the published records of prey taken by Giant Eagle Owls, the diversity would exceed that recorded for any other southern African owl.

WHITEFACED OWL

Unlike the Giant Eagle Owl, the White-faced Owl specialises in a much narrower range of prey. It feeds almost exclusively on small rodents, especially the multi-mammate mouse; in one analysis of Whitefaced Owl pellets, 95 percent of the 135 prey items identified consisted of this species. Insects may be taken, and an occasional bird, but mice are its staple diet.

In many rodent populations (especially of multimammate mice) numbers fluctuate dramatically from year to year, in some years reaching plague proportions. Whitefaced Owls respond to changing prey densities by moving around a lot. They may be absent from an area for years, and then suddenly be there in numbers, advertising away their presence by their distinctive hooting. In 1992 there was such an influx into the suburbs of Pretoria, and seven injured birds from that area were brought to a rehabilitation centre for treatment in a two-week period, whereas in previous years none had even been reported. (Barn Owls also react to rodent-population irruptions, specifically by laying larger clutches than usual; see page 32.)

There are many places where Whitefaced Owls are permanently resident. A famous Whitefaced Owl stakeout has long been the Nossob Camp in the Kalahari Gemsbok National Park, where a pair has lived for decades. They are tame and confiding, and can often be found by following the crowd of photographers queueing to take pictures of them!

Whitefaced Owls share the attributes of other *Otus* owls (the scops owl group) in having slim bodies and long ear tufts, being strictly nocturnal, and in hiding during the day by appearing as small as possible, with ears erect and eyes closed to narrow slits. Being considerably larger than Scops Owls (200 g, compared to the Scops Owl's 65 g), they are usually easier to locate and, unlike Scops Owls, will fly off rather than allow a close approach.

Much of what is known about the behaviour and nesting habits of Whitefaced Owls is the result of a study done 20 years ago by two schoolboys in Harare for the Young Scientist's Exhibition (see 'Further Reading', page 84). They found the female owl to be slightly larger than the male, and the sexes distinguishable by the amount of white visible on the chest and belly (the male owl was

lighter, with a central white streak running down his front which the female lacked). They established that the incubation period lasted 30 days, and that the female did most of the incubation, during which time she was fed by the male. The pair that they studied nested three metres up in the fork of a tree, a commonly used nest position. Old stick nests of small raptors (such as Gabar Goshawks, Little Banded Goshawks or Blackshouldered Kites) are also used, as are old Grey Lourie nests, these often being so skimpy that the eggs can be seen through the nest from below.

Above: By drawing its feathers in tightly, a Whitefaced Owl avoids detection. Bottom: A typical clutch of Whitefaced Owl eggs.

In years of rodent abundance Whitefaced Owl pairs may nest within 200 metres of each other. The main breeding period for these owls is August and September but, depending on prey availability, they may nest at any time. In one remarkable year the Nossob pair bred three times, each time successfully. If all else fails, Nossob is a good place to go for Whitefaced Owls!

THE HABITAT SPECIALISTS

All owls have special qualities, so selecting a few as being 'especially special' is done at the risk of committing a grave injustice to those excluded. But these four habitat specialists – the Barred Owl, Wood Owl, Cape Eagle Owl and Pel's Fishing Owl – are definitely not run-of-the-mill owls, and their relative scarcity endows them with a reciprocal degree of desirability among the ranks of birders.

Far left: Barred Owl.
Above: Young Pel's Fishing Owl.

THE HABITAT SPECIALISTS

The species considered in this chapter do not have much in common with each other beyond their ranges in southern Africa being more restricted than those of other owls, and their habitat requirements more specific than most.

BARRED OWL

The Barred Owl – the smallest of the four – is a species of taxonomic intrigue. It is a *Glaucidium* owl, and therefore built much like a Pearlspotted Owl, but it is about a third larger (110 g versus 75 g). It also lacks the nape spots ('false eyes') found in many owls in this genus.

White, spotted underparts and dark, barred upperparts characterise the Barred Owl.

Six or seven isolated populations of Barred Owl 'lookalikes' occur across the African continent, from West Africa to the Eastern Cape. In some reference books these have been given specific status (for example, the Chestnut Owl, Ngami Owl, Scheffler's Owl and Albertine Owl), while in others they are all regarded as versions of a single Barred Owl species. The call notes of the birds across this range do not differ greatly, lending support to the latter interpretation.

From a southern African perspective, the occurrence of Barred Owls in the Eastern Cape province is especially intriguing. The population is very small, and the birds here are virtually impossible to find. Separated by 800 kilometres from the next nearest population of Barred Owls, they also differ somewhat in looks and calls from the more northerly populations of this species. The intrigue stems from the prospect that they may be a distinctly different species, and from not knowing why they are so rare and elusive – just the sort of project to challenge a resourceful researcher!

The first two Barred Owl specimens were collected in the Eastern Cape in the early 1800s and formally described in 1834. These specimens differ from the more northerly Barred Owls by having darker brown, less distinctly barred wings and back, and a spotted rather than barred head. For more than a century they constituted the only specimens of

A Barred Owl arrives at its nest to feed its chicks with a small nocturnal snake.

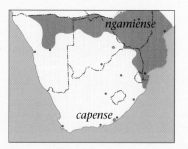

ngamiense

capense

A small large-headed owl; white below, spotted and barred with brown; warm brown above, barred with paler brown. Prominent white wing stripe. No ear tufts. Small barred face with bright yellow eyes. Call, a series of mellow purring notes. Length 210 mm.

the nominate race of the Barred Owl, *Glaucidium capense capense*. (The population of less-dark-plumaged birds that extends northwards from the Kruger National Park into Zimbabwe and Botswana belongs to the race *ngamiense*, sometimes also referred to as the 'Ngami Barred Owl'.)

For about 150 years there were no further signs of Barred Owls in the Eastern Cape. Then, in 1980, one was picked up dead on a garden lawn at Kenton-on-Sea, and following this lead a handful of sightings have since been made there. No nesting or other behaviour has yet been described, but bird photographer John Carlyon, who followed up the Kenton-on-Sea discovery, found and photographed a pair of birds and tape-recorded their calls. These calls, he found, differed from the calls of Ngami Barred Owls by being slower and uttered with longer intervals between phrases. This does not prove nor disprove that the two races are specifically distinct, but it does hint at the possibility.

WOOD OWL

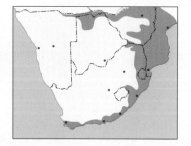

A medium-sized owl; dull brown on the head, wings and back, spotted and streaked with white; barred rufous-and-white below. Off-white face with dark brown smudges around the eyes; dark brown eyes and red-rimmed eyelids; no ear tufts. Call, a rippling hoot. Length approximately 350 mm.

Barred Owls often prey on insects such as millipedes, crickets, grasshoppers and moths.

Barred Owls also occur in small numbers in northern KwaZulu-Natal and it has been convention to treat these as part of the same *capense* population as the Eastern Cape birds, despite their wide geographic separation. Carlyon followed his discovery in the Eastern Cape by searching for Barred Owls in Mkuze Game Reserve in KwaZulu-Natal – and he found them there, calling not like *capense* birds but like Ngami birds!

The place to go to see Barred Owls is not the Eastern Cape nor northern Kwa-Zulu-Natal, but the Okavango region, where they are especially common in stands of tall mopane woodland and galleries of riparian trees along watercourses. This is also their typical habitat in Zimbabwe and in the lowveld of eastern South Africa. They are not birds of indigenous forest (at least, not in southern Africa), but do seem to require a woodland of tall trees with a well-developed canopy. Their occurrence in the Eastern Cape appears confined to euphorbia-clad hillsides and valleys.

Despite their local abundance in northern Botswana, relatively little is known about the habits and behaviour of Barred Owls. They are especially active at dusk and dawn, and hunt by watching the ground from a low perch. During a six-hour photographic session at a nest near the Kruger National Park one of us (RE) recorded 40 visits made to bring food to nestlings. Prey appeared to consist mostly of insects (praying mantises, millipedes, crickets, grasshoppers and hawk moths), and three small snakes were also brought in. This nest, like others we have seen and others described in references, was in a natural cavity created by a branch having broken off the main trunk of a tree; it was 200 mm deep and four metres off the ground. Unlike Pearlspotted Owls, Barred Owls appear not to make use of woodpecker holes and their nests are consequently less easy to discover.

At dusk Barred Owls announce their presence with a purring call of six to eight syllables ('kroo-kroo-kroo...'), or a rocking, two-syllabled 'prr-purr' call, repeated several times. Calling can often continue through the night and may extend into the day. Most calling is associated with the onset of the breeding season in August. In the absence of their calling, they are not easy birds to locate.

WOOD OWL

The year 1834 marked the introduction to the world's bird catalogues not only of the Barred Owl but also of the Wood Owl. Its type specimen was collected, appropriately (because the Wood Owl is a true forest owl), in the Knysna forest, where it still occurs commonly. Wood Owls are found in afromontane forests

A Wood Owl shows its characteristic yellow beak.

(such as that at Knysna), coastal forests (such as that in northern KwaZulu-Natal and Mozambique) and in riparian forests that line many of the larger rivers of northeastern South Africa, Zimbabwe, northern Botswana and the Caprivi. In all these habitats they can be very numerous.

Detecting the presence of Wood Owls at night is easy, because they are particularly vocal owls, but finding them in the day is another matter. Their call is a

The underwing markings of a Wood Owl, recorded for research purposes.

delightful chuckle
of six to eight syllables ('woo-ho, hu hu
hu hu hoo'), with the male and female
often calling in tandem, her call higher
pitched than his. Interspersed with the
chuckle you may often hear another,
higher-pitched, yowling note ('eee-
yow'); this is uttered by the female.

As is the case with other owl species,
Wood Owls are particularly vocal in the
month or two before breeding, and
between July and September resident
pairs may call, at intervals, all night. They
are usually very responsive to playbacks
of their calls, and a survey using playback
done by ornithologist Alan Kemp along
the Levubu River in the Kruger National
Park revealed that the riparian gallery
here supported a pair about every 600
metres (23 pairs in total along 15 kilometres of river).

Wood Owls are strictly nocturnal, and
they are rarely seen in daylight unless
disturbed from their daytime hideaway or
flushed from a nest. They are sedentary
and highly territorial. Pairs remain

Top left: Cape Eagle Owl nestling.

together, and the partners in a pair roost
close together during the day, finding a
spot in the leafy canopy of a tree where
they are concealed by a tangle of creepers
or thick foliage. Once such a site is
located (and if the birds are not
disturbed), they can be found there day

Above: Pel's Fishing Owl, fresh from a plunge, watches the water below for fish movement.

after day, calmly gazing down at the observers. Finding them is the trick, however, as whitewashed branches and pellets are not easily detected in the confines of a dark forest.

Similarly, Wood Owl nests are not easy to locate, although the sites chosen are often only a few metres off the ground. In most cases Wood Owls lay their eggs in a hollow in a tree trunk, either where a branch has fallen off, leaving a cavity, or in the top of a broken-off stump, usually within two to four metres of the ground. Very occasionally they may lay in the old

CAPE EAGLE OWL

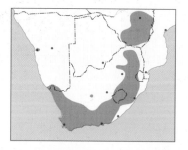

A large, stocky owl, with prominent ear tufts and large, bright orange eyes. Richly patterned upperparts with rufous on the head, back and wings. Chest boldly blotched with rufous, black and white; white throat patch; barred belly and leggings. Huge talons. Call, a deep, resonant hoot. Males most vocal in the months leading up to breeding (April, May and June). Length 580 mm.

nest of a bird of prey, in which case they will be high up in a tree, or they may lay on the ground at the base of a tree. They are very secretive when nesting, and the nest site can easily be overlooked.

Once you've found a Wood Owl nest, however, you can check it year after year with a very good chance of finding the birds again, as they reuse nest sites annually. An example of these birds' extraordinary attachment to a nest site has been described in Zimbabwe where, despite two females being shot in successive years on the nest, and six successive clutches of eggs being collected from it, nesting at the site continued year after year!

A clutch of two eggs (occasionally one or three) is usually laid. The incubation, done by the female, lasts approximately 31 days. During this time the female can become remarkably confiding and may have to be lifted by hand if you want to examine the eggs.

Wood Owls have been found to be mainly insectivorous, taking a variety of such prey items as crickets, beetles, hawk moths, cicadas, caterpillars and grasshoppers. Mice and shrews are less frequently taken, and, even more occasionally, birds and snakes. Peter Steyn's nest observations have shown that the parents hunt and bring food to their chicks throughout the night, but with the greatest frequency in the first few hours after dark.

The chicks remain confined to the nest for about 30–37 days and thereafter remain with the parents for a further three to four months, giving away their presence in the forest by making a wheezy, asthmatic 'see-e-e-e' whenever they get hungry.

A family of Cape Eagle Owls at their nesting ledge on a rock face. During the breeding season most of the owls' activities are focused near the nest.

CAPE EAGLE

The third of the 'specials' is the Cape Eagle Owl, a large, boldly marked bird built in the stocky mould of the other eagle owls, and with huge talons, large eyes and prominent 'ears'.

Cape Eagle Owls occur in a series of isolated populations restricted to the highland areas that run the length of the African continent between the southern Cape and Ethiopia in the north. The southernmost 'island' population is that found in South Africa; these are known as the true 'Cape' Cape Eagle Owls (race *capensis*), and they are smaller than those found elsewhere on the African continent. They frequent rocky, usually mountainous, areas and they are nowhere common except, perhaps, in the cold, high-lying interior of the Drakensberg and Maluti mountains.

Moving north, the next Cape Eagle Owl population occurs in Zimbabwe, and the larger size of these birds has led to their being designated to another race, known locally as 'Mackinder's Eagle Owl' (race *mackinderi*). Mackinder's Eagle Owls extend northwards from here, via the high-lying areas of Malawi and Tanzania, into East Africa. A third race is found north of this, in the highlands of Ethiopia.

These different forms of the Cape Eagle Owl are regarded as being the African representatives of the world's largest owl, the Horned Owl-Eagle Owl superspecies, which extends across Eurasia and the Americas.

Mackinder's Eagle Owl is 20 percent larger than the nominate Cape Eagle Owl, and the difference in the size of prey taken by the two is striking.

Cape Eagle Owl parent and chick.

Val Gargett, an ornithologist who spent many years studying Black Eagles and other raptors in Zimbabwe's Matobo Hills, showed that the Matobo owls preyed mainly on red rock hares, animals with an average weight of 2,3 kg, whereas the Cape Eagle Owls studied by South African ornithologist David Allan in the escarpment region of Mpumalanga took a very wide diversity of items, but mainly rats and mice (up to 350 g in weight). Both races occasionally took formidably large prey; at Matobo, infant klipspringer and duiker were recorded as prey, while in Mpumalanga, guineafowl and Bald Ibises were taken, as were four other species of owl!

Separated by the low-lying Limpopo valley, the two southern African eagle owl races do not overlap in range and there is no way of knowing whether they would interbreed under natural conditions, since they never come into contact in the wild. A keen Zimbabwean birder, John Jones, suggests that the calls of the two are different, and that Mackinder's Eagle Owl does not respond to playbacks of the Cape Eagle Owl's calls, whereas it does respond to playbacks of its own call.

In the light of this, a comparative DNA study of the two could well add another owl species to southern African avifauna.

Cape Eagle Owls breed in winter and their deep, resonant hooting can be heard on a clear night from a distance of several kilometres. Males call in this way in the lead-up to breeding; April, May and June are their most vocal months, and this is the best time of the year for locating the birds by call. For the duration of the breeding period (which lasts about four months) the owls' activities are focused near the nest, and the surrounding rocks become increasingly marked with their white, viscous, toothpaste-like droppings. A careful scan of a potential nesting cliff for a concentration of such markings is the most rewarding way of locating both the birds and their nests.

The nest is a shallow scrape in the ground, usually on a ledge, and usually overhung by rock or screened by vegetation from above. Sometimes the site chosen is inaccessible without a rope, and seems more suited to, say, a Jackal Buzzard. More often, though, the nest scrape is located on a small, easily scalable rock face to which any predator can easily gain access.

These sites are reused year after year, and prey remains, especially small bones, accumulate here in quantities (Cape Eagle Owl nest sites have been often referred to as 'ossuaries' for this reason). Dave Allan, collecting prey debris at 17 nest sites in Mpumalanga, was able to obtain a record of 480 different prey items.

Like other larger owls, pairs appear to breed not every year, but at two-yearly intervals. Even during the non-breeding years, however, the pair is likely to be found in the vicinity of their nest site during the winter breeding months, and their nest scrape is often freshly prepared, as if laying were about to begin.

PEL'S FISHING OWL

From cold highlands to steamy, mosquito-ridden lowlands, the move from the preferred habitat of the Cape Eagle Owl to that of Pel's Fishing Owl could hardly be more extreme. Pel's is the largest of three species of fishing owl that occur in Africa, and it is the only one that reaches southern Africa, furtively staking its claim along forest-lined rivers in the hottest, lowest-lying parts of the subcontinent.

In southern Africa, Pel's Fishing Owl is best known from the Okavango system, and it is thought that about 100 pairs occur in this 1,5 million-hectare wetland. Its high profile in this region is due partly to film-maker Tim Liversedge's research on them here, including his stunning video *Haunt of the Fishing Owl*, and

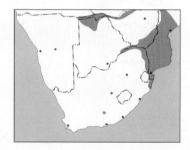

PEL'S FISHING OWL

A very large, warm orange-coloured bird; darker above than below, and scalloped and spotted above and below with black. No ear tufts. Large, inky black eyes. Call, a deep, resonant hoot. Length approximately 360 mm.

Pel's Fishing Owl is strictly nocturnal. During the day it hides in densely foliaged trees along watercourses.

partly because the birds occur regularly at several popular tourist destinations (Jedibe Island and Shakawe, for example) where they can easily be seen.

In addition to being exciting birds to observe in the wild, Pel's Fishing Owls really are remarkably interesting. Their eyes are inky-dark and seemingly bottomless. They have bare legs and toes (which would seem more at home on an Osprey than an owl), and the toes have sharp, spiny bases. They almost lack the facial disc that characterises the owl family, and they also do not have downy edges to their flight feathers, so when flushed they fly off not silently, but rather noisily. Not that you will see these birds flying about much during the day – they are strictly nocturnal, and from dawn to dusk they sit quietly in the thickest, darkest spots along a river.

On the positive side, their preference for areas with the largest, most densely foliaged trees along forested river margins does narrow down the options somewhat in a search for Pel's Fishing Owls. Roosting birds often hide within the canopy of trees such as the Natal mahogany and the Low-veld mangosteen. Undisturbed roosts are used repeatedly and signs of the birds' presence – their ginger-coloured feathers, faeces, fish bones, fish scales and the odd fish head too large to swallow – are usually to be found below such sites. When put to flight, these owls often alight farther along the river in the bare branches of a dead tree to watch the proceedings, rather than diving away into another dark hideout.

Pel's Fishing Owls subsist almost entirely on fish, mostly in the size range 100–500 g, and chiefly comprising catfish of various species. Occasionally other items, such as small crocodiles, frogs and crabs, are taken but these are incidental to their staple diet of fish. The owls fish the rivers from perches (dead stumps, overhanging branches and emergent rocks) that overlook sections of quiet or slow-flowing water, usually positioned within a metre of the water's surface. They sit quietly in such spots, sometimes for hours on end, and when prey is sighted they plunge after it feet first. Their spiny feet are clearly adapted for holding onto slippery fish; and because of the nature of their prey, a silent approach (and hence silent flight) is not a necessity.

In normal circumstances pairs are dispersed at intervals along rivers, each pair centring its activities on a section of the river where there are suitable roosting and nesting sites as well as hunting perches overlooking the water. During drought conditions, when many rivers cease flowing and the river's water is reduced to a series of pools, this territorial dispersion may be forsaken and, at night, you may find several birds gathered around a single pool to hunt. In particularly severe conditions some rivers may have to be abandoned altogether, with the birds moving into unfamiliar country to survive. This would be our explanation

Above: The typical nest site of a Pel's Fishing Owl – a large hole in a fig tree. Opposite: Pel's Fishing Owl showing its heavily barred upperparts.

for the most unusual sighting of a Pel's Fishing Owl made in 1987 by Eastern Cape birder Joan Collett in the Karoo, in an area hundreds of kilometres outside its normal range.

In the early 1990s wildlife researcher Keith Begg and others systematically surveyed the rivers of the Kruger National Park for Pel's Fishing Owls. The largest numbers of birds were located along two of these, the Olifants (about 15 pairs along its 100-kilometre length within the park) and the Levubu (six to 12 pairs, depending on water flow, along 23 kilometres of river), with a few additional pairs on other, smaller rivers. The flow in both the Olifants and the Levubu rivers has been seriously impaired by water abstraction higher up in their catchments, and the long-term negative effects of this on the region's owls is a cause for great concern. Not only has there been a definite impact on the

seasonal availability of surface water and the fish populations in these rivers, but the riparian forest in which the owls roost and nest may not, over a period of time, be sustainable as a direct result of the diminished water supply.

For the time being, however, these owls have a haven in this park, and they can even be seen, if you are lucky, from the tourist roads. The territory of one pair extends along the river directly below the Olifants Rest Camp, and at dawn and dusk these birds are sometimes to be seen from the lookout here; another pair's territory runs past Balule Rest Camp. If nothing else, you may hear their deep, resonant hoot, ending abruptly, from these camps in the dead of night: 'hooomm-hut', repeated every ten or twenty seconds.

Breeding occurs after river flow has peaked, and February, March and April are the main egg-laying months in both the Kruger National Park and the northern Okavango populations. As in the case of other large owls, pairs breed, on average, at two-yearly intervals, raising a single chick at a time. Nests are invariably in large trees which either have a hollow formed where a branch has broken off or where several branches diverge from the main trunk, providing a spacious bowl. Most nest sites in the Kruger National Park have been in sycamore figs, whereas those in the Okavango are usually in a crotch in the main stem of a jackalberry. One or two eggs are laid, the incubation period is thought to last about 33 days, the nestling period 68–70 days and post-fledging dependence a further four to seven months – all figures that accord with what is expected for a large owl.

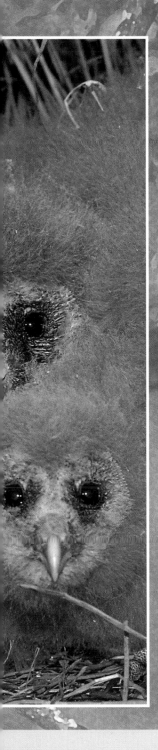

HANDS-ON OWLING

In a world increasingly modified by man, owls are subject to impacts that did not exist a few centuries ago – poisoning, loss of habitat, loss of safe nest sites, road deaths – to name a few. As a result, dead, sick and injured owls are more commonly encountered by the layman than are live ones. This chapter offers solutions to some of the problems facing owls, as well as ideas for research, and techniques that are useful when photographing owls.

Far left: A hissing brood of Grass Owl chicks.

HANDS-ON OWLING

Most people see fewer live owls than dead or injured ones – flattened corpses on the tarmac, a bundle of feathers hanging on a barbed-wire fence, a row of stricken-looking birds on a perch in a rehabilitation centre or zoo, all casualties of manmade hazards that affect owls. Owls face many natural hazards anyway, but piled on top of these are the growing perils of living in an environment increasingly modified by man. Many of these changes have already been touched on – water abstraction and its impact on rivers frequented by Pel's Fishing Owls and overgrazing of marshes that support Grass Owls, for instance. While some threats are species-specific, however, others are more general.

Birds of prey, by their very nature, are particularly susceptible to being poisoned,

Road casualty – a Barn Owl struck at night by a passing car.

either inadvertently when they feed on prey that has itself been poisoned, or when they take poisoned bait intended either for themselves or for another predator. The demise of many southern African eagles and vultures through poisoning has been well documented, and it is now becoming increasingly clear that owls are suffering a similar fate. For man, poison is a quick, effective way of dealing with a rodent problem, whether it be rats or mice in the house or gerbils in the farmlands. Owls, however, are particularly vulnerable to rodenticides (poisons designed to kill rodents) because they prey to such a large extent on rodents.

The impact on owl numbers of this kind of secondary poisoning can be enormous. Karen Trendler, who runs a wildlife rehabilitation centre at Pretoria, has reported that about 40 percent of the thousand-odd sick or injured owls brought in over a recent three-year period (1995-1997) were victims of secondary poisoning. This owl mortality could be prevented, or at least minimised, firstly, if the rodenticide chosen were non-toxic to birds (see box on page 73), and secondly, if all poisoned rodent carcasses were collected and safely disposed of.

If a sick owl (one that cannot fly, or responds slowly) is found, suspect poisoning. Some other cause (such as a bacterial infection or viral attack) may be responsible, but because of the prevalence of poison usage in the environment, it is

Spotted Eagle Owl chicks, often 'rescued' off the ground to their detriment.

very probable that poison is involved. Symptoms of a poisoned bird include paralysis in its legs, mucus in its mouth and eyes, diarrhoea, and a body temperature that fluctuates between high and low. Such birds will almost certainly die if left to their own devices, but they stand a good chance of recovery if not too far gone and if correctly treated and looked after. There are many animal/bird hospitals and rehabilitation centres in southern Africa, and your best response is to get the bird to one of these as soon as you can. If this is not possible, you should nonetheless phone them to get specific advice on how to treat and care for the sick or injured owl. In such cases the bird's symptoms need to be described in detail so that a correct diagnosis can be made.

Treatment in the case of owls poisoned with rodenticides or organophosphates involves rehydrating the bird for 24 hours (with an electrolyte such as Ringer's lactate, applied with a syringe or tube) to get its kidneys working to flush the toxins, then introducing it to a diet of white meat before getting it back to its more usual diet. Severe cases, such as those poisoned by queleatox, may be treated with atropine, but the use of this antidote carries the risk of overdosing.

What should be done with a sick or injured owl?

• Pick up the bird from behind (to avoid being clawed by its talons), using a towel to cover its head.
• Check its symptoms so that they can be reported to a rehabilitation centre. Is it obviously injured? Is it bleeding from

USING RODENTICIDES SAFELY

Rodenticides, whose active ingredients may include brodifacoum, bromodiolene, ditenacoum, dimethialone, or flocoumaten, should not be used in situations where the dying rodents could possibly come into contact with owls, as these constituents have been implicated in owl mortality as a result of secondary poisoning.

There are at least three commercially available rodenticides which appear to be 'owl-safe'. One (Racumin) has coumatetralyl as an active ingredient, while the other two (Rinoxin and Avirat) contain warfarin.

Wherever possible, place the rodenticide inside a container (for example, a box or carton with a small access hole cut for the rodent) so as to minimise its accessibility to other potential victims. Make it routine procedure after putting out any rodenticide to collect all the carcasses of rodents that have been poisoned, and dispose of them safely.

any orifice? Can it walk? Is it breathing slowly or fast? Is it gasping for breath? Is it hot or cold? What are the colour and state (dry or moist) of its eye and mouth membranes? Are its faeces normal, watery or tarry? Does its breath smell bad? Has it regurgitated food?

- Confine the bird in a dark box (a carton will do) with air holes; a piece of carpet on the floor will prevent it from sliding around. Never use cotton wool, as this may get into the bird's eyes, and don't use a wire cage, which may damage its beak if it tries to escape. Leave the bird in an undisturbed position.
- Don't attempt to force-feed the bird.
- Phone a vet for instructions, and get the bird to a vet or wildlife rehabilitation centre as soon as possible.

Nest boxes often attract owls to gardens. Here a Barn Owl box is under construction.

What should be done with abandoned owl chicks?

Because young owls leave their nests before they can fly, they are sometimes, when found, assumed to be orphans and 'rescued'. Big mistake! If at all possible such chicks, provided they are not sick or injured, should be returned to the site where they were discovered. Once it is dark their parents will re-establish contact and continue feeding them, even after an absence of a day or two. (If the chicks are in a garden and threatened by pets, temporarily fence them in, or the pets out.)

Hand-raising owl chicks is in itself not difficult but, for the uninitiated, preventing them from imprinting on humans and teaching them to hunt once mature are often insurmountable obstacles. Imprinted birds (that is, those that 'think'

ADVICE ON SICK OR INJURED OWLS

Botswana: Mokolodi Wildlife Foundation, Gaborone. Tel. (09267) 31-1414
Namibia: NARREC. Tel: (061) 26-4409.
South Africa: National Wildlife Rescue Hotline. Tel: (012) 808-1106, (012) 808-0592 or (082) 920-3627.
Zimbabwe: Larvon Bird Garden, Harare. Tel: (04) 21-0216. Chipangali Wildlife Orphanage, Bulawayo. Tel: (09) 7-0764.
In addition to providing advice on what to do with the bird, they will direct you to the nearest or the most appropriate rehabilitation centre.

they are human as a result of being exposed only to humans during infancy) and birds incapable of hunting successfully are essentially doomed in the wild. Rehabilitation is about getting birds fit and back into the wild where they belong, not keeping them as glorified pets. If it is impossible to return such chicks to the custody of their parents, they should be handed over to a rehabilitation centre where they stand a good chance of being correctly raised and eventually successfully released back into the wild.

Above: Barn Owl drowned in a farm dam. Bottom right: Barn Owl box on a chimney.

What should you do if you find a dead owl?

All southern Africa's natural-history museums maintain collections of bird specimens, and additions to these collections are invariably welcomed. If the bird is freshly dead and in good condition it can be mounted; otherwise, it could be used as a study skin or a skeletal specimen, providing researchers with study material, or for DNA sampling.

Before doing anything, however, take the opportunity of having a close-up look at the bird. Notice the downy fringes to its flight feathers, and lift the facial feathers around and behind its eyes to see its large ear openings. Check the bird's legs to see

if it is ringed; if it is, remove the ring, flatten it and post it to SAFRING (University of Cape Town, Rondebosch, 7700, South Africa). Include a covering letter detailing the exact locality the bird was found (its GPS – geographic positioning system would be the ideal!), the date it was found, your name as the collector and the suspected cause of death (write 'unknown' if you don't have any idea).

If the dead Barred Owl found at Kenton-on-Sea in 1980 had not been dispatched in a plastic bag to the Durban Museum, this species would probably still be considered extinct in the Eastern Cape. For this reason, write all this information on a label, too, and attach this to the dead bird's leg, then seal it in a plastic bag and keep it in a deep freeze until such time as it can be delivered to a museum, for the attention of the bird curator.

How can owls be attracted to gardens, farms and villages?

Managing a habitat to suit owls is seldom a realistic option, given their considerable spatial requirements and their diverse prey needs. Maintaining an owl-friendly environment is achievable, however, particularly with respect to ensuring that only bird-safe pesticides are used there.

Providing nest sites for owls is often a productive habitat-management option. With the exception of the two grass-living owls, all other species depend to a greater or lesser extent on natural cavities or nests built by other birds. Putting up boxes for Barn

Barn Owl peering out of its nest box.

Owls is frequently successful and indicates that their occurrence is often limited by a lack of suitable nest sites. Artificial boxes also work for Spotted Eagle Owls, Wood Owls, Pearlspotted Owls and Scops Owls, provided they are tailored to imitate the natural situations preferred by these species. If any of these species occur in the area where owl encouragement is being considered, putting up appropriate nest boxes could be rewarding.

Because of their close association with man, providing homes for Barn Owls and Spotted Eagle Owls is especially appropriate, and these can be attached to the walls of existing buildings or trees in a way that harmonises with the environment. Our recipe for a Barn Owl box is one with floor dimensions of 600 mm x 400 mm and front and back wall heights of 400 mm and 500 mm respectively (differing so as to give a sloping roof to the box and thus

Above: Contents of box: chicks and eggs.

such as a seldom-used outbuilding away from traffic and flow of people, and where it is inaccessible to predators.

Swarms of bees may pose a hazard to Barn Owls as they sometimes take over their nest boxes, causing the birds to abandon eggs or chicks and flee. If you are on the spot when such a swarm arrives, the bees can be discouraged from settling in by burning a mosquito coil at the entrance to the box. The owls will return once the bees have departed.

Barn Owls often hang around buildings at night, whether or not there are nest sites in them, and they can become a problem when they choose to perch during the night on exposed trusses, furnishings or wall-hangings in open verandas. Within a few days the accumulation of whitewashing on the floor below can be spectacular! The only effective way of preventing this is to remove anything that may provide a perch for the owls, or make the perches unattractive to them, or cut off access to these perches by closing off the veranda at night with shade cloth. Once the habit is broken, the probability is that the bird will not return; if it does, repeat the exercise.

Because Spotted Eagle Owls have smaller broods than Barn Owls, a nest box for this owl can be smaller (floor dimensions of 400 mm x 400 mm are fine). Spotted Eagle Owls favour nesting in more exposed situations, so instead of an entrance hole, one of the sides of the box should be a 'half-wall', closing off only the bottom part. The box can be attached to the side of a building, or a few metres up against a large tree trunk, or on a large horizontal tree branch.

allow rain to run off). The entrance hole (100–120 mm in diameter) should be placed in the middle of one side and can be round or square. Such a box is easily and cheaply constructed using treated slats or split poles. A piece of wood just below the box's entrance is useful for the birds to perch on when arriving, and a waterproof lining to the roof is essential. The taller side of the box should be firmly attached to a wall or tree trunk, in a quiet position,

What research projects can be done on owls?

People with a special interest in owls can undertake all sorts of interesting projects on them, either on their own or by collaborating with a research group.

The Avian Demography Unit at the University of Cape Town runs several bird data collection projects that include information on owls. For example, they have a nest-record programme in which details of nesting attempts made by owls can be recorded. The Unit also undertakes the administration of all bird ringing in South Africa and can be approached for information on who to contact and how to go about ringing owls (ringed Spotted Eagle Owl recoveries are often made, and thus offer a good return on effort). The Unit also has a project underway to survey bird fauna in all conservation areas, and any information on owls from such places would be a useful contribution to this programme.

You don't have to become involved in such cooperative projects in order to do interesting and meaningful research, however. Once again, the Barred Owls in the Eastern Cape offer an example. Here is a study crying to be done, and all that is required is the answers to straight-

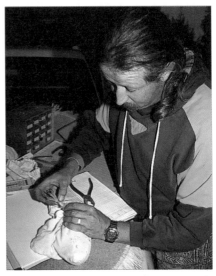

A Barn Owl in the process of being ringed during a bird data collection project.

forward questions about where the birds occur, population sizes, what particular features of their habitat are crucial to their survival, where they nest, and how successful their breeding efforts are. The answers to these would have great conservation relevance for the species.

Another project would be to investigate the use of owls in the traditional-medicine or 'muti' trade. Visit a cross-section of shops to see how many owl carcasses are on sale and what species are sold, and find out where these came from, what they are used for and how much they sell for.

WHERE TO TAKE OWL SPECIMENS

Bloemfontein National Museum.
tel: (051) 447 9609.
Cape Town South African Museum.
tel: (021) 24 3330.
Durban Durban Natural Science
Museum. tel: (031) 300 6220.
East London East London Museum.
tel: (0431) 43068.
Pretoria Transvaal Museum.
tel: (012) 322-7632.
Windhoek The State Museum of
Namibia. tel: (061) 293-4437.
Bulawayo Zimbabwe National
Museum. tel: (09) 60045.

Collecting pellets of the Spotted Eagle Owl for analysis. Much can still be learnt about owls and their prey by examining pellets.

From time to time you may see a request in a bird-club magazine from research staff at universities and museums for information or participation in an owl project, such as to report nest sites or collect pellets. Despite the many analyses that have already been done, there is still much to be learnt about owls and their prey by examining their pellets. One of many possibilities in this regard would be to track the changing composition of the prey taken by a single pair of owls in an area by collecting their pellets at regular intervals (daily, weekly or monthly) and analysing these batch by batch.

PHOTOGRAPHING WILD OWLS

A number of good books and innumerable popular articles have been written about bird photography, covering such aspects as choice of cameras, lenses and films, stalking techniques, the use of hides and photography at the nest. (For a list of some of these, see 'Further Reading' on page 84.) There is no need to cover all this ground again, so this chapter concentrates on what makes photographing in the dark different from photographing in the day.

A limited amount of daytime photography of wild owls is possible, especially if a roosting bird's exact whereabouts are known. Some species will allow a close approach during the day, for example, a roosting Whitefaced Owl (see page 55), provided this is done slowly and sensitively, and with frequent pauses if the bird shows unease (watch especially for foot or eye movements which signal agitation).

The opportunities offered by such photography are limited, however. A roosting bird approached in this way will be static (and probably anxious, with feathers drawn in and eyes closed to narrow slits), while the use of a hide to photograph owls at a nest during the day is usually disappointing because very little happens until nightfall. Daytime photography is further limited because roosting owls often hide themselves inside dense foliage and perch high above the ground.

At night, when owls are on the move, the best photo opportunities involve setting up at a position the bird is likely to fly to and settle at. This can be at a nest, at a perch en route to the nest or at a perch where bait has been placed to lure the bird in. Such photography usually calls for the use of a hide, and for careful preparation during the preceding day.

As with all bird photography, the use of hides requires sensitivity to the bird's responses: the hide must be built with materials that are wholly opaque (this is especially important at night, when a light may be used inside the hide); it must be

A Pearlspotted Owl nest log with a hide in place for photography.

Focus is also enhanced by setting the lens aperture to give the maximum possible depth of field (in the f11–f22 range). To achieve this, the flashes should be fairly close to the subject (less than five metres away), and if they are attached to the hide you can work comfortably with a smallish telephoto lens (300 mm or less). A zoom lens in the 100–300 mm range is particularly useful in providing flexibility for framing the picture.

Illuminating the bird is conventionally done using flash. It is preferable to use two flash heads in order to reduce hard-shadow areas in the picture, and these should be clamped into position (on, say, the hide frame) on either side of the lens, one level with the lens and the other raised about 45°. This balances the lighting on the subject. The flashes should be situated at least 250 mm away from the lens to prevent a red-eye effect. (If they are too close to the lens, the light reflects off the owl's retina into the lens and creates the

pinned tightly closed so that it does not flap and, if it is set up at a nest, it should gradually be moved up to the nest from a distance, preferably over a couple of days, so as to accustom the bird to its presence. The hides we use are metal-framed, with floor dimensions of about 1 m x 1 m and a height of 1,5 m, covered with thick, dark-coloured cloth.

The two main difficulties with night photography of owls are focusing on and lighting the subject. For focusing we use a thin light beam controlled by a dimmer switch (run off a 12-volt battery) so that the amount of light can gradually be increased or decreased. We also start by covering the beam with a red filter, and later, if the birds are relaxed, we remove this (focusing is much easier when done in white light). We direct this light beam at the position where the bird is expected, clamping the torch into position before-hand so as to minimise the need for movements which the owl may hear.

The inside view of a nest showing a Pearlspotted Owl arriving with prey.

red-eye effect.) 'Red eye' can also be minimised – if the bird is confiding and does not react to white light – by turning up the light from the beam controlled by the dimmer switch; the owl reacts to this light by closing down its pupils, and this cuts down the reflection off its retina. Flash does no damage to an owl's eyes, although it can dazzle the owl temporarily. The flashes should be powered by a battery that can run without interruption for the duration of the photo session (up to six hours), and this battery should be placed inside the hide where it can easily be switched on or off.

To minimise errors, familiarise yourself with your flashes before embarking on such photography. Run tests with the flashes beforehand to determine the angles and distances that give the best results. Do these tests at night using a 'dummy' bird (perhaps a feather duster) positioned against the type of background you'll be dealing with in the field.

Because of the silent flight of most owl species, the approach of a bird to the nest or perch is often not detected, and the first you know of its presence is the soft thud you hear as it alights. Choosing a moonlit night for photography improves your chances of seeing the approaching bird before its arrival, but to get flight pictures by relying on your reflexes is often a hit-and-miss affair.

A variety of home-made infrared-beam trigger releases have been developed by night-photography enthusiasts to overcome this obstacle. In such set-ups an infrared beam is strategically positioned across the flight path used by the bird en route to its nest, and the camera is triggered when the beam is broken (sometimes by the owl, sometimes by some other creature!). This allows you to sit in the comfort of your car, watching proceedings from a distance. From time to time details of how to build such equipment are given in photography magazines, and one such reference is listed under 'Further Reading'.

A final factor for successful owl photography at night is to be prepared for long sessions in the hide. Have a comfortable, padded stool to sit on (one that doesn't squeak at your every move!), have the camera set at a comfortable height, be warmly clothed and know exactly where all the items you may need (torch, film, camera batteries, etc.) are so that you can find them in the dark. Have a notebook and pen at the ready for recording observations or camera settings. Wear clothing that doesn't rustle when you move (natural fibres are better than synthetics). Wear protection against mosquitoes and other potential irritants so that you don't have to slap or scratch in the hide.

Be quiet and still; move as little as possible, preferably not at all. Let your eyes become accustomed to the outside ambience. If you are in elephant or lion country, make sure you have a back-up person, and work out a distress-signalling system with him or her beforehand!

The 'red-eye effect' is created when flashes are situated too close to the camera lens.

GROUP	BEGINNERS' OWLS		OWLS IN THE GRASS		BUSHVELD OWLS	
COMMON NAME	BARN OWL	SPOTTED EAGLE OWL	MARSH OWL	GRASS OWL	SCOPS OWL	PEARLSPOTTED OWL
SCIENTIFIC NAME	*Tyto alba*	*Bubo africanus*	*Asio capensis*	*Tyto capensis*	*Otus senegalensis*	*Glaucidium perlatum*
LENGTH	320 mm	450 mm	360 mm	360 mm	170 mm	180 mm
WEIGHT Unsexed birds / Males / Females	330 g	590 g / 690 g	320 g	420 g	65 g	76 g / 62 g / 95 g
COLOUR MORPHS		grey: common brown: rare			grey: common brown: rare	
EYE COLOUR (Iris)	dark brown	yellow: common orange: rare	dark brown	dark brown	yellow	yellow
CALL (Most frequent)	screech	hoot	rasping croak	click	purr	whistle
PREY Mainly	rats, mice, moles, shrews	mice, bats arthropods, shrews, birds, lizards	mice, arthropods, shrews	rats, mice, shrews	arthropods	arthropods
Incidental	lizards, birds		birds, lizards, frogs	birds		mice, birds, frogs, lizards, shrews
PELLET SIZE (where known)	45 x 25 mm	65 x 25 mm		50 x 25 mm		
BREEDING SEASON Main egg-laying months	early winter (Mar-May)	early summer (Aug-Sept)	early winter (Mar-May)	early winter (Mar-May)	early summer (Sept-Oct)	early summer (Sept-Oct)
Range of months	all months	Jul-Feb	all months	all months	Aug-Nov	Aug-Nov
CLUTCH SIZE Usual / Range	6 / 2-19	2 / 1-5	3 / 2-5	4 / 3-5	3 / 2-4	3 / 2-4
EGG SIZE (mm)[†] Average / Maximum / Minimum	39,1 x 31,3 / 43,1 x 34,5 / 36,0 x 28,9	49,1 x 41,1 / 54,2 x 44,4 / 47,1 x 39,1	40,0 x 34,1 / 43,0 x 36,0 / 37,9 x 32,4	41,8 x 34,1 / 45,3 x 35,8 / 39,0 x 31,3	29,5 x 25,4 / 32,2 x 27,0 / 28,0 x 23,7	31,0 x 25,8 / 33,8 x 27,2 / 28,0 x 24,0
INCUBATION PERIOD	32 days	31 days	29 days	32 days	25 days	29 days
NESTLING PERIOD (from hatching) to leaving nest / to flying	50 days (same)	±21 days / 40 days	14-18 days / ±35 days	±35 days / ±42 days	±27 days (same)	30 days (same)
POST-FLEDGING DEPENDENCE		±6 weeks		±4 weeks		
% OF SOUTHERN AFRICA IN WHICH RECORDED*	38,9%	48,2%	14,2%	5,5%	21,5%	31,7%

* Figures from 'Southern African Bird Atlas'

BUSHVELD OWLS		THE HABITAT SPECIALISTS				
GIANT EAGLE OWL	WHITEFACED OWL	BARRED OWL	WOOD OWL	CAPE EAGLE OWL	CAPE EAGLE OWL	PEL'S FISHING OWL
Bubo lacteus	*Otus leucotis*	*Glaucidium capense*	*Strix woodfordii*	*Bubo capensis* race *capensis*	*Bubo capensis* race *mackinderi*	*Scotopelia peli*
620 mm	250 mm	210 mm	350 mm	500 mm	580 mm	630 mm
1 700 g 2 600 g	200 g 250 g	110 g 122 g	300 g	950 g 1 250 g	1 300 g 1 600 g	2 200 g
dark brown	orange	yellow	brown	orange	orange	dark brown
hoot	hoot	purr	hoot	hoot	hoot	hoot
birds, mammals (esp. hedgehogs), frogs, snakes, arthropods	mice, shrews	arthropods; mice, birds, lizards	arthropods; mice, birds, lizards, frogs	rats, mice, shrews; birds, insects, frogs, bats	rock hares, dassies; rodents	fish; frogs, crabs, mussels, crocodiles
100 x 40 mm			20 x 10 mm			40 x 20 mm
winter (Jun-Aug) March-Sept	early summer (Aug-Oct) Feb-Nov	early summer (Sept-Oct)	early summer (Aug-Oct) Jul-Nov	winter (May-Jul) May-Sept	winter (May-Jul) May-Sept	late summer (Feb-Apr) Jan-Oct
2 1-2	2 2-4	3 2-3	2 1-3	2 1-3	2 1-3	2 1-2
62,9 x 54,0 67,5 x 54,0 58,0 x 48,0	38,8 x 32,3 41,5 x 33,3 37,0 x 30,4	32,6 x 27,3 34,0 x 28,0 30,0 x 26,0	43,4 x 37,6 46,0 x 40,5 40,0 x 35,5	53,0 x 45,0 54,5 x 46,8 52,0 x 42,2	58,2 x 47,0 60,7 x 48,4 55,0 x 44,0	61,7 x 51,7 65,1 x 53,5 58,8 x 49,2
38 days	30 days	±30 days	31 days	38 days	35 days	33 days
±62 days ±84 days	23 days 32 days	±32 days (same)	±34 days (same)	±45 days ±75 days	±65 days	±70 days
±17 weeks	±8 weeks		±16 weeks	±25 weeks	±7 weeks	±25 weeks
14%	18,7%	8%	8,6%	6%	6%	2,5%

† Figures from *Roberts' Birds of Southern Africa*

FURTHER READING

Allan, DG. 1995. The diet of the Cape Eagle Owl. *Journal of Raptor Biology* 10: 12–27.

Angel, H. 1982. *The Book of Nature Photography.* Ebury Press, London.

Bunn, DS, Warburton, AB and Milson, RDS. 1982. *The Barn Owl.* Poyser, London.

Bunning, LJ. 1993. *The Bird Ringer's Guide.* Witwatersrand Bird Club, Johannesburg.

Coetzee, CG. 1972. 'The Identification of Small Mammal Remains in Owl Pellets'. *Cimbebasia* A2:53–64.

Dalton, S. 1982. *Caught in Motion: High-Speed Nature Photography.* Weidenfeld & Nicolson, London.

De Graaff, G. 1981. *The Rodents of Southern Africa.* Butterworths, Durban.

Erasmus, RPB. 1992. 'Notes on the Call of the Grass Owl *Tyto capensis*'. *Ostrich* 63:184–185.

Freethy, R. 1992. *Owls: A Guide for Ornithologists.* Bishopgate Press, Hildenborough.

Fry, CH, Keith, S and Urban, EK. 1988. *The Birds of Africa* (volume 3). Academic Press, London.

Gibbon, G. 1991. *Southern African Bird Sounds* (set of six tapes). Southern African Birding cc, Durban.

Harrison, JA, Allan, DG, Underhill, LG, Herremans, M, Tree, AJ, Parker, V and Brown, CJ. 1997. *The Atlas of Southern African Birds*, Birdlife South Africa, Johannesburg.

Hosking, E and Newberry, C. 1945. *Birds of the Night.* Collins, London.

Kemp, AC and Calburn, S. 1987. *The Owls of Southern Africa.* Struik Winchester, Cape Town.

Kemp, AC and Kemp, MI. 1989. 'The Use of Sonograms to Estimate Density and Turnover of Wood Owls in Riparian Forest'. *Ostrich* supplement 14:105–110.

Lecos, PJ. 1996. 'High-Speed Nature Action'. *Outdoor Photographer,* August 1996:70–73.

Liversedge, TN. 1980. 'A Study of Pel's Fishing Owl *Scotopelia peli* Bonaparte 1850 in the Panhandle region of the Okavango Delta, Botswana'. *Proceedings of the Fourth Pan-African Ornithological Congress*:291–299.

Liversedge, T. 1992. *Haunt of the Fishing Owl* (30-minute video). Tim Liversedge Productions, Botswana.

Maclean, GL. 1993. *Roberts' Birds of Southern Africa* (sixth edition). Trustees of the John Voelcker Bird Book Fund, Cape Town.

Martin, G. 1990. *Birds by Night.* Poyser, London.

Mendelsohn, JM. 1989. 'Habitat Preferences, Population Size, Food and Breeding of Six Owl Species in the Springbok Flats, South Africa'. *Ostrich* 60:183–190.

Mikkola, H. 1983. *Owls of Europe.* Poyser, London.

Newman, K. 1995. *Newman's Birds of Southern Africa.* Southern Books, Johannesburg.

Payne, RS. 1971. 'Acoustic Location of Prey by Barn Owls (*Tyto alba*)'. *Journal of Experimental Biology* 54:535–573.

Pitman, CRS and Adamson, J. 1978. 'Notes on the Ethology and Ecology of the Giant Eagle Owl *Bubo lacteus*'. *Honeyguide* 95:3–23 and 96:26–43.

Read, M and Allsop, J. 1994. *The Barn Owl*. Cassel PLC, London.

Sinclair, JC, Hockey, PAR and Tarboton, WR. 1997. *Sasol Birds of Southern Africa*. Struik, Cape Town.

Sliwa, A. 1994. 'Marsh Owl Associating With Blackfooted Cat'. *Gabar* 9:23–24.

Skinner, JD and Smithers, RHN. 1990. *The Mammals of the Southern African Subregion* (2nd edition). University of Pretoria, Pretoria.

Steyn, P. 1982. *Birds of Prey of Southern Africa: Their Identification and Life Histories*. David Philip, Cape Town.

Steyn, P. 1984. *A Delight of Owls: African Owls Revisited*. David Philip, Cape Town.

Trendler, R and Hes, L. 1994. *Attracting Birds to Your Garden in Southern Africa*. Struik, Cape Town.

Vernon, CJ. 1972. 'An Analysis of Owl Pellets Collected in Southern Africa'. *Ostrich* 43:109–124.

Worden, CJ and Wall, J. 1978. 'Observations on the Whitefaced Owl *Otus leucotis* at Cleveland Dam, Salisbury'. *Honeyguide* 94:31–37.

The small, yellow-eyed Barred Owl.

GLOSSARY

Atropine: an antidote for poisoning by pesticide.

Avian: pertaining to birds.

Avifauna: the bird component of fauna.

Binocular vision: vision that provides a three-dimensional image.

Biome: the broadest division of a continent into natural units that share common ecological processes, fauna, flora and climate.

Courtship: in birds, activity between male and female that establishes and maintains the pair bond.

Crepuscular: active at dusk and dawn.

Crop: in a bird, a food storage area in the oesophagus (between the bill and stomach).

Diurnal: active during the day.

Echolocation: detection of objects by emitting a sound and analysing returning echoes.

Families (in a taxonomic sense): a subdivision within hierarchical classification of living things that is above level of genus and below level of order.

Habitat: a particular environment inhabited by a particular species.

Incubation: the process whereby heat is applied to an egg, usually by the parent bird sitting on it, to promote embryonic development.

Mob/mobbing: noisy demonstration by small birds to the presence of a dangerous predator.

Nestling period: the period in the life of a young bird between hatching and first leaving the nest.

Nocturnal: active at night.

Nomadism: descriptive of the movements of a species that are not seasonal or cyclic.

Organophosphates: a pesticide, a phosphate-based organic compound.

Queleatox: the trade name of an organophosphate poison (known as fenthion) that is used in controlling the Redbilled Quelea.

Raptor: a predatory bird (specifically belonging to either the order of Strigiforme or Falconiforme.

Riverine: fringing a river (refers to a plant community found there).

Sedentary: descriptive of a species that does not undertake extensive movements.

Southern African region: the region south of the Zambezi and Kunene rivers.

Superspecies: a grouping of closely related species that have allopatric ranges.

Taxa: (plural of taxon) refers to a grouping at any taxonomic level (e.g. owls can be referred to as a taxon, as could Spotted Eagle Owls).

Taxonomy: the science of classification of living organisms.

Type specimen: the single or original specimen on which the description of a species is based.

INDEX